KS3 ENGLISH IS EASY

(GRAMMAR, PUNCTUATION AND SPELLING)

THE
REVISION
SERIES

www.How2Become.com

As part of this product you have also received FREE access to online tests that will help you to pass Key Stage 3 ENGLISH
(Grammar, Punctuation and Spelling).

To gain access, simply go to:

www.PsychometricTestsOnline.co.uk

Get more products
for passing any test at:

www.How2Become.com

Orders: Please contact How2Become Ltd, Suite 14, 50 Churchill Square Business Centre, Kings Hill, Kent ME19 4YU.

You can order through Amazon.co.uk under ISBN 9781910602966, via the website www.How2Become.com or through Gardners.com.

ISBN: 9781910602966

First published in 2016 by How2Become Ltd.

Copyright © 2016 How2Become.

All rights reserved. Apart from any permitted use under UK copyright law, no part of this publication may be reproduced or transmitted in any form or by any means, electronic or mechanical, including photocopying, recording, or any information, storage or retrieval system, without permission in writing from the publisher or under licence from the Copyright Licensing Agency Limited. Further details of such licenses (for reprographic reproduction) may be obtained from the Copyright Licensing Agency Ltd, Saffron House, 6-10 Kirby Street, London EC1N 8TS.

Typeset for How2Become Ltd by Anton Pshinka.

Disclaimer

Every effort has been made to ensure that the information contained within this guide is accurate at the time of publication. How2Become Ltd is not responsible for anyone failing any part of any selection process as a result of the information contained within this guide. How2Become Ltd and their authors cannot accept any responsibility for any errors or omissions within this guide, however caused. No responsibility for loss or damage occasioned by any person acting, or refraining from action, as a result of the material in this publication can be accepted by How2Become Ltd.

The information within this guide does not represent the views of any third party service or organisation.

CONTENTS

THE
REVISION
SERIES

UNDERSTANDING THE CURRICULUM

THE NATIONAL CURRICULUM

State-funded schools use a set curriculum of 'core' subjects, to form their students' timetables. These subjects are essential for providing knowledge and key skills, both of which are paramount to creating well-rounded and educated citizens.

In Key Stage 3 (ages 11-14), the core subjects that must be taught in schools include the following:

- **English**
- **Maths**
- **Science**
- **Art and Design**
- **Citizenship**
- **Computing**
- **Design and Technology**
- **Languages**
- **Geography**
- **History**
- **Music**
- **Physical Education**

All schools, Key Stage 1 to Key Stage 4, must also teach Religious Studies to their students; and from the age of 11, children will also be taught Sex Education. However, parents are given the option of pulling their children out from Religious Studies and Sex Education.

THE IMPORTANCE OF ENGLISH

Students are taught the importance of English via spoken language, reading, writing and vocabulary. Not only is this a core subject which all students are required to undertake, but this subject is an integral part of other school subjects. Children will need to have a strong grasp of the English Language, and this will prove vital if they are to be successful across their school subjects.

<u>The fundamental aims of the English subject include:</u>

- Reading with fluency and ease;

- Demonstrating a good understanding of the English Language;

- Highlighting the importance of reading, and allowing students to read for both pleasure and academia;

- Appreciate the English Language and its heritage;

- Acquire a strong English vocabulary to improve students' knowledge in regards to reading, writing and listening;

- Ability to write effective literature, adapting their writing and language in order to meet a specific purpose, context and audience;

- Improve children's confidence in their English abilities, allowing them to become competent in the English Language via verbal and written communication.

In Key Stage 3, the English subject focuses on four main 'disciplines':

- **Reading;**

- **Writing;**

- **Grammar and Vocabulary;**

- **Spoken English.**

The aforementioned disciplines are all used in order to teach students vital skills for both academia and the outside world.

READING AND WRITING

Reading and writing are extremely important basic skills, which every person should gain from an early age.

The ability to read is necessary across other school subjects too, and therefore it is important that students are able to read fluently and effectively.

Writing is a great skill which can be altered to reflect different contexts, purposes and audiences. In Key Stage 3, students are required to write different literary texts, for different purposes. Thus, this requires a strong level of knowledge regarding vocabulary and grammar.

GRAMMAR AND VOCABULARY

Students in Key Stage 3 will need to extend knowledge which was obtained in Key Stage 2.

Teachers will need to enhance students' knowledge, by teaching them the importance of grammar, punctuation and spelling. These key areas allow students not only to analyse literary texts, but also to improve their own writing style.

Linguistically, students will need to develop a strong understanding of English terminology, and learn how this can be applied to literary texts. This includes learning the ability to use appropriate vocabulary and understanding the meaning of words and phrases; and learning the ability to analyse, practice and apply literary techniques to their own work.

SPOKEN ENGLISH

Not only is written communication an important aspect of the English Language, but the ability to speak fluent English is just as vital.

Spoken English is used every day, in a range of different contexts. Developing a person's speaking skills will allow for well-rounded citizens, who have the ability to communicate effectively.

Speaking skills allow students to become more confident at speaking out loud, and to engage with the English Language competently and effectively.

Having a strong understanding of the English Language will allow students to become fluent in written and spoken English. This will allow them to communicate effectively with the world around them, thus allowing children to become engaged in cultural, social and economic issues, and intellectual debates.

ENGLISH SUBJECT CONTENT

Below I have broken down the aims and objectives of each 'discipline' for the subject. This will hopefully give you some idea of what will be assessed, and how you can improve different areas in your reading, writing and speaking abilities.

READING

Pupils will be taught how to:

❑ Develop an appreciation of the English language.
❑ Engage with a variety of literary texts including:
  - *Non-fiction, fiction, plays and poetry. Texts that cover a wide range of genres, eras, authors, styles and narratives.*
  - *Reading books for pleasure and academia.*
  - *Understanding the importance of Shakespeare's works.*
❑ Engage with challenging texts by:
  - *Learning new vocabulary, grammar and literary techniques.*
  - *Analysing key words and phrases.*
  - *Making inferences and assumptions based on the information provided.*
  - *Knowing the meaning behind the text, including the purpose, audience and context.*
❑ Read critically:
  - *Recognising different literary techniques.*
  - *Analysing narration, characterisation, style, themes and genre.*
  - *Comparing two or more texts (cross-examination).*
  - *Understanding meaning through figurative language, word choices, structure and conventions.*

WRITING

<u>Pupils will be taught how to:</u>

❑ Write with fluency, ease and control.
❑ Write a range of different literary texts including:
   ▪ *Strong, persuasive, narrative essays.*
   ▪ *Short stories, plays, poetry.*
   ▪ *Imaginative writing.*
   ▪ *Formal letters.*
   ▪ *Scripts and presentations.*
❑ Plan, draft and proofread writing:
   ▪ *Plan and draft your ideas. Think about:*
      o *Characters, narrative, themes, motives, style, context, audience, purpose.*
   ▪ *Carefully choosing grammar and understanding the importance of vocabulary.*
   ▪ *Structuring your writing format in a clear and concise manner.*
   ▪ *Understanding the importance of audience, and how your writing can be influential.*
❑ Be original and creative.
❑ Use the English language in a way that is expressive, creative, informative, imaginative or personal.

SPOKEN ENGLISH

<u>Pupils will be taught how to:</u>

❑ Verbally communicate to a high standard by:
   ▪ *Speaking confidently, persuasively and effectively.*
❑ Improve their speaking skills by engaging with particular grammar and vocabulary:
   ▪ *Understanding what type of spoken English you should use and in what context.*
   ▪ *Understanding how to get your point across in the best possible way.*
❑ Participate in verbal debates, discussions and presentations.
❑ Improve on speaking skills such as volume, tone, enthusiasm and interaction.

GRAMMAR AND VOCABULARY

Pupils will be taught how to:

❑ Improve on pre-existing grammar and vocabulary skills taught in Key Stage 2.
❑ Understand the importance of grammar:
  - *How this creates meaning.*
  - *The impact this has on the audience.*
❑ Analyse key words and phrases:
  - *Why they are used.*
  - *The meaning behind them.*
  - *What is the author implying/inferring?*
❑ Understand what grammar and vocabulary to use. Think about:
  - *What kind of literary text you are writing/reading.*
  - *What do words mean and how can they be interpreted?*
  - *Is it a formal or informal piece of literary text?*

English is not only a core subject, but a topic that impacts upon every aspect of our daily lives. As you can see, it is imperative that students are able to engage with the English Language, in order to improve on vital skills and knowledge.

USING THIS GUIDE

This guide focuses specifically on Key Stage 3 English grammar, punctuation and spelling. This book will focus on the basics that every child will need to know, to ensure top marks across the English subject.

REMEMBER – It's really important that you have a good grasp of grammar, punctuation and spelling; no matter what subject you are learning.

By the end of this guide, you will have a strong knowledge regarding the following:

ADJECTIVES	NOUNS	PRONOUNS	VERBS	ADVERBS
PHRASES	CLAUSES	TENSES	CONNECTIVES	ARTICLES
SILENT LETTERS	ACTIVE	PASSIVE	STANDARD ENGLISH	MISUSED WORDS
PLURALS	PREFIXES	SUFFIXES	STRUCTURE	COMMAS
BRACKETS	COLONS	SEMI-COLONS	HYPHENS	SPEECH MARKS

HOW WILL I BE ASSESSED?

In Years 7, 8 and 9, children will be assessed based on Levels. These 3 years do not count towards anything, and are simply a reflection of progression and development. Key Stage 3 (Years 7, 8 and 9) are schooling years which determine whether or not pupils are meeting the minimum requirements. These 3 years are integral for preparing pupils for their GCSEs (which will begin in Year 10).

Although these years do not count towards any final results, they do go a long way to deciphering which GCSEs you will pick up in Year 10. For example, if you were excelling in Art and Design in KS3, you could consider taking this subject at GCSE. The subjects that you choose at GCSE will impact upon your future aspirations, including future education and career opportunities.

You will be monitored and assessed throughout these schooling years, via the following:

• Ongoing teacher assessments;
• Term progress reports;
• Summative assessments at the end of each academic year.

By the end of Key Stage 3, pupils are expected to achieve Levels 5 or 6.

THE
REVISION
SERIES

INCREASE YOUR CHANCES

Below is a list of GOLDEN NUGGETS that will help YOU and your CHILD to prepare for the Key Stage 3 English.

Golden Nugget 1 – Revision timetables

When it comes to revising, preparation is key. That is why you need to sit down with your child and come up with an efficient and well-structured revision timetable.

It is important that you work with your child to assess their academic strengths and weaknesses, in order to carry out these revision sessions successfully.

TIP – *Focus on their weaker areas first!*

TIP – *Create a weekly revision timetable to work through different subject areas.*

TIP – *Spend time revising with your child. Your child will benefit from your help and this is a great way for you to monitor their progress.*

Golden Nugget 2 – Understanding the best way your child learns

There are many different ways to revise when it comes to exams, and it all comes down to picking a way that your child will find most useful.

Below is a list of the common learning styles that you may want to try with your child:

- **Visual** – the use of pictures and images to remember information.
- **Aural** – the use of sound and music to remember information.
- **Verbal** – the use of words, in both speech and writing, to understand information.
- **Social** – working together in groups.
- **Solitary** – working and studying alone.

Popular revision techniques include: *mind mapping, flash cards, making notes, drawing flow charts,* and *diagrams.* You could instruct your child on how to turn diagrams and pictures into words, and words into diagrams. Try as many different methods as possible, to see which style your child learns from the most.

> *TIP – Work out what kind of learner your child is. What method will they benefit from the most?*
>
> *TIP – Try a couple of different learning aids and see if you notice a change in your child's ability to understand what is being taught.*

Golden Nugget 3 – Break times

Allow your child plenty of breaks when revising.

It's really important not to overwork your child.

> *TIP – Practising for 10 to 15 minutes per day will improve your child's reading ability.*
>
> *TIP – Keep in mind that a child's retention rate is usually between 30 to 50 minutes. Any longer than this, and your child will start to lose interest.*

Golden Nugget 4 – Practice, practice and more practice!

Purchase past practice papers. Although the curriculum will have changed for 2016, practice papers are still a fantastic way for you to gain an idea of how your child is likely to be tested.

Golden Nugget 5 – Variety is key!

Make sure that your child reads a VARIETY of different literary texts. Broadening their understanding of different genres, styles and formats will help them prepare effectively for reading comprehension.

> *TIP – Take your child to a library and let them discover different types of books. This will greatly increase their understanding of different literary styles.*

Golden Nugget 6 – Improve their confidence

Encourage your child to communicate verbally, as well as in writing. This will allow them to improve their confidence and improve their spoken English.

> *TIP – Have discussions and debates in order to encourage your child to open up and discuss their views.*
>
> *TIP – Try and get your child to deliver presentations to family members and friends. This will really help to improve their confidence.*

Golden Nugget 7 – Stay positive!

The most important piece of preparation advice we can give you, is to make sure that your child is positive and relaxed about assessments.

Don't let the exams worry you, and certainly don't let them worry your child.

> *TIP – Make sure the home environment is as comfortable and relaxed as possible for your child.*

Golden Nugget 8 – Answer the easier questions first

A good tip to teach your child is to answer all the questions they find easiest first. That way, they can swiftly work through the paper, before attempting the questions they struggle with.

TIP – Get your child to take a practice paper. Tell them to fill in the answers that they find the easiest first. That way, you can spend time helping your child with the questions they find more difficult.

Spend some time working through the questions they find difficult and make sure that they know how to work out the answer.

Golden Nugget 9 – Make sure they refer back to the text

One of the biggest mistakes a child can make in their assessments, is that they don't refer back to the text. All of the answers can be found in the text, therefore they should support their answers with information taken from the passage, as opposed to relying on their memory.

Golden Nugget 10 – Understanding key terms

The next section is a glossary containing all the KEY TERMS that your child should familiarise themselves with.

Sit down with your child and learn as many of these KEY TERMS as you can.

TIP – Why not make your child's learning fun? Write down all of the key terms and cut them out individually. Do the same for the definitions.

Get your child to try and match the KEY TERM with its definition. Keep playing this game until they get them all right!

Golden Nugget 11 – Check out our other revision resources

We have a range of other English resources to help you prepare for EVERY element of KS3 English.

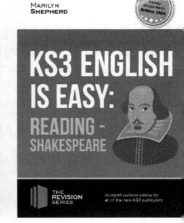

ABSTRACT NOUN	A word used for an idea that is not part of the physical world (i.e. love or anxiety).
ACTIVE SENTENCES	A sentence in which the subject acts.
ADJECTIVE	A 'describing' word. A word used to describe what something *looks, feels, smells* or *tastes* like. Adjectives also tell us how someone is *feeling*.
ADVERB	Adverbs are words that describe a verb. These words tend to tell us *how* something is being done, or give more information on *what* is being done.
ALLITERATION	The repetition of the same sound or letter, used at the beginning of adjacent or closely connected words.
AMBIGUOUS	Having more than one possible interpretation.
ANTAGONIST	The enemy of the protagonist.
ANTITHESIS	Opposites.
ANTONYM	An antonym refers to a word which has the **opposite** meaning to another.
APOSTROPHE (')	An apostrophe is a punctuation mark used to (1) indicate belonging or (2) to show letters have been omitted, which forms a contraction. *(See contractions.)*
ASSONANCE	Repetition of vowel sounds, in the middle of words.
AUDIENCE	A group of people who will view a text.
AUTHOR	The writer or creator of that particular literary text.
CHARACTERISATION	The way in which a writer scripts their character. This is done through speech, action and interaction with other characters.
CHARACTERS	The people that appear in a literary text.

CLAUSE	A clause is a part of a sentence that contains a verb and a subject.
CLIMAX	The point at which the text reaches its greatest moment of suspense. Often the main crisis.
COLLECTIVE NOUN	A noun for a group of the same thing.
COLLOQUIAL	Popular informal writing (colloquialism).
COLON **(:)**	A punctuation mark used to (1) join sentences, (2) introduce lists, (3) introduce a quotation or (4) introduce explanations.
COMMA **(,)**	A punctuation mark used to (1) indicate a pause between parts of sentences or (2) to separate items into a list format.
COMMON NOUN	Word for a thing that is not a name.
COMPARISON	Similarities and differences between different texts.
CONCRETE NOUN	Word for a physical thing (e.g. bike)
CONJUNCTION	A conjunction is a word that joins phrases or words together.
CONTEXT	Identifying meaning of the literary text, based on the use of words, the time it was written, circumstances and situation.
CONTRACTION	Contractions are 'shorthand' ways of writing words. It is one word usually made up of two words. *For example, the word 'don't' is made up of the words 'do' and 'not'.*
COUNTER ARGUMENT	Opposing views of the argument.
DASH **(–)**	A dash is used to separate information. It is stronger than a comma, but not as formal as a colon. Not to be confused with a hyphen (a dash line is longer).
DERIVATION	Where something (a word) comes from.

DETERMINER	A determiner is a word that goes before a noun in order to clarify it.
DIALOGUE	Spoken speech (a conversation) between two or more people.
ELLIPSIS (...)	An ellipsis is a set of three dots (full stops) which can (1) add suspense, (2) leave a sentence hanging or (3) show interruptions or missing words.
EVIDENCE	A way of supporting your answers by using ACTUAL proof from the passage.
EXCLAMATION MARK (!)	An exclamation mark is used to show a command or something that is forceful or surprising.
FACT	True pieces of information.
FICTION	A literary style in the form of prose (novels). These events and people are imaginary – it is invented / not from real life.
FIGURATIVE LANGUAGE	A figure of speech that goes beyond the literal meaning. *For example, metaphors, similes, hyperbole, personification.* Figurative language is used metaphorically.
FIRST PERSON	Style of narrative from one character's viewpoint (e.g. I).
FULL STOP (.)	A full stop should be used to end a sentence.
HOMONYMS	These are words that *sound* and are *spelled* the same, but have different meanings.
HOMOPHONES	These are words that *sound* the same but are spelt differently, and have different meanings.
HYPERBOLE	Exaggeration of ideas, not meant to be taken literally, but used as a way of emphasising something.

IAMBIC PENTAMETER	Verse of five pairs of syllables, each having an unstressed syllable followed by a stressed syllable.
IMAGERY	Visually descriptive or figurative language.
INFERENCES	A conclusion based on evidence and reasoning.
INVERTED COMMAS (" ")	Inverted commas are used to show direct speech or quotation. These can either be single (') or double ("). Inverted commas can also be used to draw attention to something unusual, ironic or arguably incorrect.
IRONY	Suggesting a meaning by saying the opposite of what is actually meant.
LANGUAGE	The way in which something is written or communicated.
LEGENDS	An old form of literature. A combination of myth and historical fact to describe a hero or figure.
METAPHORS	Words or phrases used to make comparisons between people, objects, places or animals.
MNEMONIC	A memory technique.
MODERN LITERATURE	Texts written or based in the contemporary period.
MYTHS	Ancient stories about how the world was created, the natural world and the spiritual truths. They also refer to ideas or beliefs that are untrue.
NON-FICTION	Writing that is based on true / real-life events or facts. It provides the reader with real and factual information.
NOUN	A word that names something.
ONOMATOPOEIA	Words that sound like what they are describing.
OPINIONS	Statements that might not be true. They are based on personal beliefs and personal thoughts.

OXYMORON	Two contradictory ideas used together (e.g. bitter sweet).
PARAGRAPHS	A way of breaking up text, in order for the passage to flow better. Each paragraph usually deals with a different theme or idea. Indicated by a new or indented line.
PASSIVE SENTENCES	One in which the subject is acted on.
PATHOS	Emotional appeal.
PEE	Point, evidence, explanation.
PERSONIFICATION	Giving human or personal characteristics to inanimate objects.
PLAYS	A type of literary style which involves dialogue between characters. Often intended for theatrical productions.
PLURAL	More than one of something. Opposite to 'singular'.
POETRY	A style of literary work which is based on feelings and ideas; using styles, rhythms, verses and composition.
POSSESSIVE PRONOUN	Stating ownership (e.g. his or hers).
PREDICTIONS	A way of guessing or forecasting what *could* or *might* happen in the future.
PREFIX	A prefix is added to the beginning of a word to make a new word.
PREPOSITION	A preposition tells us where something is or how they are related.
PRESENTATION	The way something is portrayed to its readers / audience.
PRONOUN	A word that replaces the noun.
PROSE	A natural flow of written or verbal speech.

PROTAGONIST	The hero/heroin of a story.
QUESTION MARK (?)	A question mark is used to indicate a question.
RELATIVE PRONOUN	Used in subordinate sentences, in a clause referring to the main clause (e.g. which, who).
REPETITION	The act of repeating something that has already been said or written. Used for effect to emphasise a point.
RHETORICAL QUESTION	A question that doesn't require an answer.
RHYTHM	A strong pattern of a beat, which you can hear in words.
SEMI-COLON (;)	A semi-colon is used to separate longer sentences but still reads as one complete sentence, or to link two closely related sentences.
SHAKESPEARE	An English poet and playwright who wrote important sonnets and plays.
STANDARD ENGLISH	Form of English used widely and understood by most.
STANZA	Groups of lines in a poem, almost like the paragraphs of a story.
STRUCTURE	The way a literary text is laid out. The structure of a text will depend on what *type* of text it is.
SUBJECT-VERB AGREEMENT	Grammatical matching of subject and verb (e.g. 'She WAS not' instead of 'She WERE not').
SUFFIX	A suffix is added to the end of the word to make a new word.
SYMBOLISM	The use of symbols to represent an idea or quality.
SYNONYM	A word that has the same or similar meaning to another word.

TAUTOLOGY	Accidently saying the same thing twice but in different ways.
TENSE	When something was written.
THIRD PERSON	Style of narrative which is omniscient (e.g. he or she).
TONE	The mood created by particular language.
TRADITIONAL LITERATURE	The oldest type of literature. Stories passed down from generation to generation.
VERB	A verb is a doing or action word.

THE
REVISION
SERIES

ARTICLES AND PREPOSITIONS

(Grammar)

ARTICLES

ARTICLES are words that go <u>before</u> nouns to determine whether something is <u>specific</u> or <u>general</u>.

The three most common determiners that you ALWAYS use are:

- A
- An
- The

Articles are an example of determiners. Determiners tell you whether the noun is general or specific.

<u>Using '**a**'</u>

- The word '**a**' is very generic.
- This should be used to talk about something in general, as opposed to something specific.
- You should use '**a**' when the next word starts with a <u>consonant sound</u>.

<u>Using '**an**'</u>

- '**An**' should be used when the next word starts with a <u>vowel sound</u>.

<u>Using '**the**'</u>

- The word '**the**' refers to something more specific.
- You should use the word '**the**' to talk about something in particular.

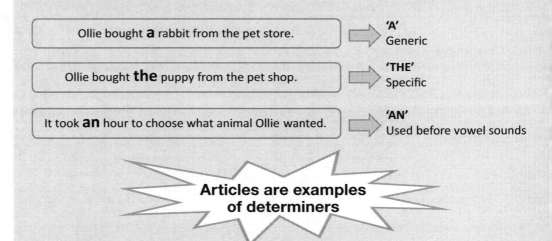

DETERMINERS

There are loads of determiners, and each are used for different reasons.

The three main reasons for using determiners:

1. To show whether something is specific or general.
2. To show who owns something.
3. To show how many things there are.

Other determiners include:

some	all	this	hers
his	every	each	those
my	yours	five	which

A determiner is a <u>short word</u> that provides some information about a noun, but doesn't describe it.

There are different types of determiners:
ARTICLES = 'a', 'an', 'the'
POSSESSIVES = 'my', 'your', 'ours', 'hers', 'his'
DEMONSTRATIVES = 'this', 'those', 'which', 'that'
QUANTIFIERS = 'two', 'three', 'every', 'each', 'some', 'all'

Vowel sounds include the following letters: a   e   i   o   u

Make sure you know when to use 'a' and 'an'. For example, 'a uniform' (although the next word starts with a vowel, it actually has the sound of 'y', so therefore this would be 'a' and not 'an'.

PREPOSITIONS

PREPOSITIONS are words that tell you where or when things happen, in relation to one another.

PREPOSITIONS TELLING YOU WHERE

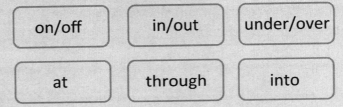

on/off	in/out	under/over
at	through	into

Examples

- He sat **on** top of the roof.
- I had to climb **through** the window.
- I jumped **over** the wall.
- I saw my cousin **at** the party.

PREPOSITIONS TELLING YOU WHEN

until	during	before/after
while	since	in

Examples

- I went on holiday **during** the summer holidays.
- **After** dinner, I went outside to play.
- I had to stay indoors **until** it stopped raining.
- It had been a long time **since** I saw my grandad.

Some prepositions can act as **CONNECTIVES**.
Check out the connectives chapter for more information!

PREPOSITIONS are used to indicate:

- **Time**
- **Location**
- **Direction**

Question 1

Insert 'THE', 'A' or 'AN' into the following sentences.

a) _____ girl sat on _____ grass and was looking for _____ shooting star.

b) It was _____ important night for Brooke. She had planned _____ opening night for her clothing store, and she wanted it to be _____ huge success.

c) "Please, I really want _____ new battle game for my console," said Jim, who had been waiting for this game for _____ long time.

d) I went to Maidstone shopping centre and had to buy _____ new dress for my best friend's wedding.

Question 2

Below is a list of words. Write the following words in the correct part of the table. Is the word a preposition or determiner?

| through | next to | before | in front of | the | little |

| since | a | about | every | behind | its |

DETERMINER	PREPOSITION

Question 3

Using two example sentences, explain why you would use 'an' instead of 'a'.

_____

_____

EXAMPLE 1

_____

EXAMPLE 2

_____

Question 4

Work out which preposition you would use in the following sentence. Write the preposition in the crossword.

Across

2. The kangaroo jumped _____ the wall.

3. I liked playing outside _____ the winter.

5. It was _____ the point.

8. The cat sat _____-_____-_____ the fridge.

Down

1. My brother hid _____ the tree.

4. I had to come _____ because it was raining.

6. I walked _____ a lamppost.

7. The book was _____ the coffee table.

9. I hung the picture _____ my wall.

ANSWERS TO ARTICLES AND PREPOSITIONS

Question 1

a) **The** girl sat on **the** grass and was looking for **a** shooting star.

b) It was **an** important night for Brooke. She had planned **an** opening night for her clothing store, and she wanted it to be **a** huge success.

c) "Please, I really want **the** new battle game for my console," said Jim, who had been waiting for this game for **a** long time.

d) I went to Maidstone shopping centre and had to buy **a** new dress for my best friend's wedding.

Question 2

Determiners = the, a, its, every, little

Prepositions = before, behind, next to, since, through, in front of, about

Question 3

You would use 'an' instead of 'a', when the next word sounds like a vowel.

You could have written any example sentences to long as you have used 'an' correctly.

<u>For example:</u>

It was an honour to meet you.

It took an hour to get home from work.

Question 4

1. Behind   **2.** Over   **3.** During   **4.** Inside   **5.** Besides

6. Into   **7.** Underneath   **8.** On top of   **9.** On

HOW ARE YOU GETTING ON?	

THE
REVISION
SERIES

CONNECTIVES

(Grammar)

CONNECTIVES

CONNECTIVES are basic and easy to understand!

They are short words or phrases that are used to <u>join words together</u>, in order to make a sentence.

Conjunctions can also be used to <u>link</u> sentences together, in order to make them flow better. This means you don't have to keep putting a full stop and ending the sentence abruptly.

- That sentence might read better joined by the following sentence, with the use of a conjunction.

THINK of CONJUNCTIONS like a JIGSAW PUZZLE.

TYPES OF CONJUNCTIONS

Below is a list of some of the common types of conjunctions that you will need to know.

And	So	But	Yet	Because	Until
However	Since	Even though	Suddenly	As	Although
Alternatively	Meanwhile	At last	Perhaps	Nevertheless	Despite
Whenever	Furthermore	Therefore	While	Besides	Finally
In addition to	Consequently	Next	Except	Similarly	In fact
Also	On the other hand	Even so	Whereas	After all	Indeed

Question 1

Create your own sentences, using the following connectives.

But

_____

_____

While

_____

_____

Whereas

_____

_____

Until

_____

_____

Question 2

Using the connectives listed below, match up the sentences on the left with the sentences on the right. The first one has been done for you.

My brother covered his ears	because	the weather was miserable.
I finished my homework	despite	continued to eat 10 satsumas.
I sat on the sofa	until	it was really noisy.
I love my brother	but	our constant arguing.
Katie enjoyed the park	and	my mum told me to go to bed.
Henry liked monsters	yet	sending random snapchats.
Jordan wanted to lose weight	even though	I was still confused.

Question 3

Complete the sentences below, by using the correct connectives.

1. It was an important day for me _____ I was waiting for my letter regarding a job position as a doctor.

2. The clouds went black _____ we decided to head home.

3. It was getting late _____ I decided to go to bed. I had to be up very early in the morning _____ I needed to be wide awake for my busy day ahead.

4. I went to after school club _____ my brother had detention. That way, we could walk home together.

ANSWERS TO CONNECTIVES

Question 1

You can write any sentence you want, so long as you have used the connectives correctly. Get a parent or guardian to check over your sentences to make sure that they read correctly.

<u>For example:</u>

- I was asked to give a presentation **but** I hated speaking in public.
- I sung my brother a song **while** he fell asleep.
- I was good at sports, **whereas** my sister was good at academia.
- I stayed at the party **until** the very end.

Question 2

My brother covered his ears **because** it was really noisy.

I finished my homework **but** I was still confused.

I sat on the sofa **until** my mum told me to go to bed.

I love my brother **despite** our constant arguing.

Katie enjoyed the park **even though** the weather was miserable.

Henry liked monsters **and** sending random snapchats.

Jordan wanted to lose weight **yet** continued to eat 10 satsumas.

Question 3

1. It was an important day for me **because** I was waiting for my letter regarding a job position as a doctor.
2. The clouds went black **so** we decided to head home.
3. It was getting late **so** I decided to go to bed. I had to be up very early in the morning **because** I needed to be wide awake for my busy day ahead.
4. I went to after school club **while** my brother had detention. That way, we could walk home together.

HOW ARE YOU GETTING ON?

THE
REVISION
SERIES

ADJECTIVES

(Grammar)

ADJECTIVES

ADJECTIVES are words that <u>describe nouns</u>.

Adjectives give sentences extra 'flavour' and detail, which allows for descriptive writing.

Remember, **NOUNS** are words that <u>name something</u>. Adjectives transform nouns by telling you more about how something looks or feels.

So, the adjective will *describe* that something in more detail.

The girl was **tiny.**	The adjective describes the <u>*size*</u> of the girl.
The **black** dog.	The adjective describes the <u>*colour*</u> of the dog.
I was **terrified.**	The adjective describes the <u>*feelings*</u> of the noun – 'I'.

USING MORE THAN ONE ADJECTIVE

Sometimes you may want to use more than one adjective to describe something.

If you do this, these adjectives may need to be separated using commas. You would use commas if you are describing different aspects of something.

It was going to be a **long, stressful** and **tedious** journey.	See how the adjectives are describing the length of time, emotional state and boring aspects of the journey.

Adjectives that are describing the same aspect of the noun, will not need commas.

The sea was **royal blue.**	See how the adjectives are both describing the colour of the noun (sea).

TOP TIP – if you are using more than one adjective, ask yourself – are they really necessary? Sometimes, your descriptions will create more of an impact if you choose a strong, powerful adjective. Is it really necessary to use two adjectives that mean similar things?

ADJECTIVES

USING HYPHENS IN BETWEEN ADJECTIVES

Sometimes, you may need to use a hyphen in between adjectives, in order to provide a clearer meaning.

Hyphens are a punctuation mark used to join two words that are closely connected. They show which words should be read together.

> The electrical circuit had a **high-voltage**.

⇨ Without the hyphen, you could read 'high' as being high up; the hyphen makes it clearer.

> He was extremely **self-centred**.

⇨ See how the hyphen allows you to read 'self' and 'centred' as one complete word.

> It was my **brother-in-law's** birthday.

⇨ See how the hyphen allows you to read 'brother', 'in' and 'law' as one complete thing.

COMPARATIVE VS. SUPERLATIVE

COMPARATIVE ADJECTIVES are used to compare qualities of two people or things.

SUPERLATIVE ADJECTIVES are used to compare qualities of a person or thing in relation to everyone in the group.

ADJECTIVE	COMPARATIVE	SUPERLATIVE
One syllable = ending in E *Strange, cute, late*	Add 'r' *Stranger, cuter, later*	Add 'st' *Strangest, cutest, latest*
One syllable = ending in a vowel and consonant *Big, slim, hot*	Double consonant and add 'er' *Bigger, slimmer, hotter*	Double consonant and add 'est' *Biggest, slimmest, hottest*
One syllable = ending in more than one vowel or consonant *Near, fast, light*	Add 'er' *Nearer, faster, lighter*	Add 'est' *Nearest, fastest, lightest*
Two syllables = ending in 'Y' *Happy, funny, lonely*	Change 'Y' to 'I' and add 'er' *Happier, funnier, lonelier*	Change 'Y' to 'I' and add 'est' *Happiest, funniest, loneliest*
Two syllables or more = not ending in 'Y' *Beautiful, elegant, generous*	Use the word MORE before adjective. *More beautiful, more elegant, more generous*	Use the word MOST before adjective. *Most beautiful, most elegant, most generous*

Question 1

Underline ALL of the adjectives in the sentences below.

1. Tyrone was wearing a black, chequered jacket.
2. Simon was a curious boy.
3. It was the most bizarre feeling.
4. The fragile, lonely woman sat recumbent in her bed.

Question 2

Use the table below, and write the adjectives in both their comparative form and superlative form.

ADJECTIVE	COMPARATIVE	SUPERLATIVE
Bad		
Distinctive		
Little		
Clumsy		
Far		
Much		

Question 3

Explain why you would use hyphens in between adjectives. Give two example sentences demonstrating the use of hyphens.

_____

_____

EXAMPLE 1

_____

EXAMPLE 2

_____

Question 4

Eight adjectives have been taken out of their place. Write the adjectives in the spaces below, in order for the passage to read correctly.

CARELESS	NOISELESS	WRINKLY	ANCIENT
COLOURFUL	FREE	TRANQUIL	HIGH

The forest was full of [____] flowers and [____] trees.

Wildlife searched for food [____] in the tree tops. Squirrels climbed

quickly, rabbits hopped through the grass and a [____] deer peered

behind the [____] trees. The sounds of the wind whistled through the

leaves. An orchestra of birdsong filled the [____] atmosphere. Nature

roamed around the forest, [____] and [____] .

Question 5

Each statement (a-f) contains at least one adjective. Underline the adjectives in each sentence and then find them in the word search.

```
Z N H T G S X L N F K Z D Y T E Y P D Z
Q G S Z C Z S T U S L P D E S E O M E N
J V Q G U X R F V F K E C L S L U A T O
L U F S S E C C U S I H V N O L N D N Y
A N T W E L V E K J N T E E W C G S E S
F N M U I O S K Q O B M U Y N Q N F L O
W X A H K F L B L E M B U A W P J D A E
X Y G K L Y U O Q I N U K R E F K J T H
U O P V X L G T S O M M T M R B J Z P G
A W R F Q I U A C R A K M U J S B V I A
A R D U C G J S G U N I K Z H H T H L V
F Q K A C G L M L Q S D B A D H X Z G H
K H L F A N K O V T O S M A O O T A M F
T L E O W Y D G Y B P W H P H E L F O A
D N Q J V J O M E N Y F S H M W V S F E
W E N I K V W N D W M T M X I Q Z N L O
M D K L X B D Z D U X C C R O R C Q B J
Q H H D F J A E J D G H F I N C B F Y Y
F V C U F S F I C Q V P G R M N C P S Z
H J L Z F B G C M W L D W K V D N L B R
```

a. It was a beautiful morning.

b. Most technological advances are successful.

c. It was an immense feeling.

d. The talented, young actress was offered a role.

e. It was a cold, misty and damp evening.

f. There were twelve girls in the class.

Question 6

Why is it not always a good idea to use more than one adjective when describing something?

_____

_____

ANSWERS TO ADJECTIVES

Question 1

1. Tyrone was wearing a <u>black</u>, <u>chequered</u> jacket.
2. Simon was a <u>curious</u> boy.
3. It was the most <u>bizarre</u> feeling.
4. The <u>fragile</u>, <u>lonely</u> woman sat <u>recumbent</u> in her bed.

Question 2

Bad = Worse = Worst

Distinctive = More distinctive = Most distinctive

Little = Less = Least

Clumsy = Clumsier = Clumsiest

Far = Farther = Farthest

Much = More = Most

Question 3

Hyphens need to be used in between some adjectives that are closely connected, in order to provide a clearer meaning.

Your examples can be anything so long as you have used a hyphen correctly. Please get a parent or teacher to check your answers.

For example:

The blue-eyed boy was called Tommy.

Linda's daughter is getting married. She will gain a son-in-law.

Question 4

The words should be written in the following order:

Colourful, ancient, high, noiseless, wrinkly, tranquil, careless, free

It doesn't matter what way round the words 'careless'' and 'free' go.

Question 5

a. It was a <u>beautiful</u> morning.

b. <u>Most</u> <u>technological</u> advances are <u>successful</u>.

c. It was an <u>immense</u> feeling.

d. The <u>talented</u>, <u>young</u> actress was offered a role.

e. It was a <u>cold</u>, <u>misty</u> <u>and</u> <u>damp</u> evening.

f. There were <u>twelve</u> girls in the class.

Question 6

Sometimes one adjective is powerful enough to make the point you are trying to make. Sometimes, using more than one adjective negates from the point, and the words are unnecessary. Similar adjectives are often unnecessary because they are saying the same thing.

THE
REVISION
SERIES

VERBS AND ADVERBS

(Grammar)

VERBS

VERBS are '<u>doing</u>' or '<u>being</u>' or '<u>action</u>' words.

These types of words are very useful because they tell us what someone is doing or what is happening.

EVERY SENTENCE NEEDS A VERB!
SENTENCES CAN HAVE MORE THAN ONE VERB!

<u>There are two types of verbs:</u>

1. Doing words

2. Being words

'DOING' VERBS

These verbs describe an action.

> She **plays** in the garden.

> The boy **skates** once a week.

> The child **kicks** the football.

> Harry **eats** his roast dinner.

'BEING' VERBS

Being words are other types of verbs that tell you how something is.

These type of verbs come from the verb 'to be'.

> I **am** healthy.

> We **are** going on holiday.

> We **were** late for class.

> It **was** going to be a great day.

SOME VERBS ARE NOT OBVIOUS

Some verbs are not obvious:

Exist   Conclude   End   Begin   Arrive   Possess

VERBS

VERBS NEED SOMETHING OR SOMEONE TO DO THE ACTION

Verbs require a noun or pronoun to do the action being described.

The verb can be placed either before the thing doing the action, or after.

1. Sentences that tell us that someone or something is doing the action are called **active sentences.**

2. Sentences that tell us that someone or something has an action done to them are called **active sentences**.

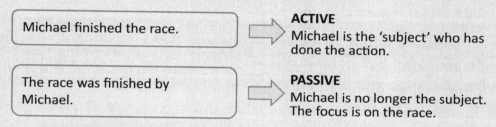

Michael finished the race.	**ACTIVE** Michael is the 'subject' who has done the action.
The race was finished by Michael.	**PASSIVE** Michael is no longer the subject. The focus is on the race.

SUBJECT-VERB AGREEMENT

Verbs need to agree with the subject. The subject is the person or thing doing the action.

In simpler terms, if a subject is singular, the verb will also need to be singular.

The **wolf live** in the woods.	**OR**	The **wolf lives** in the woods.

- The first statement is incorrect.
- The wolf is the subject and is singular.
- The verb (to live) needs to be singular – lives.

They likes going camping.	**OR**	**They like** going camping.

Which sentence is correct?

- The subjects 'they' is plural.
- There is more than one person, so the verb (to like) needs to be plural – like.

VERBS

VERB TENSES

Verb tenses are a great way to understand **when** something is happening.

REMEMBER = there are three tenses:

- Past
- Present
- Future

Verbs change depending on the tense of the sentence.

I have done a marathon.	⇒	**PAST**

I am doing a marathon.	⇒	**PRESENT**

I will be doing a marathon.	⇒	**FUTURE**

It is important that your writing remains in the SAME tense. Do not swap tenses in your writing. For example, if you begin writing in past tense, you must remain in the past tense.

For more information on tenses, please visit page 71.

ADVERBS

ADVERBS describe verbs.

Adverbs are used to tell you when or how an action was done.

Most adverbs end in 'ly' – quickly, silently, dramatically etc.
However, not all adverbs follow this rule – late

Adverbs also describe adjectives.

- *Quite, nearly, really and very are all adverbs.*

They provide extra information about the adjective – "quite big" or "really annoying".

ADVERBS VS. ADJECTIVES

Knowing what is an adjective and what is an adverb can sometimes be quite tricky.

As mentioned previously, a lot of adverbs end in 'ly'. However certain words (such as 'friendly') end in 'ly', but are actually adjectives!

Tricky right?

Words that are describing the noun will be an adjective. Words that add more information to the adjective, or tell you how or when something occurs, are an adverb.

ADVERBIAL PHRASES

You can also get **ADVERBIAL PHRASES** which work in the exact same way, but instead of using one word, use several.

- As soon as possible
- As silently as he could
- June last year
- Next year

FRONTED ADVERBIALS

Fronted adverbials are groups of words, used at the beginning of a sentence, to describe an action that follows.

Question 1

Tick the box to show whether the highlighted word is a verb, adverb or adjective.

SENTENCE	VERB	ADVERB	ADJECTIVE
It **was** my brother's birthday yesterday.			
He was a **scrawny** boy.			
It was an **old-fashioned** looking room.			
She **wrote** a short story about grief.			
The bees were **everywhere**.			
She was too **young** to understand.			

Question 2

What is an adverbial phrase? Give an **example** to support your answer.

_____

_____

_____

Question 3

For the following professions, write **two verbs** to describe the tasks that they may encounter in their job.

a) Farmer

_____

b) Scientist

_____

c) Police Officer

_____

d) Nurse

_____

Question 4

For each of the sentences below, circle whether the sentence is **active** or **passive**.

1. The horrific fire destroyed the rainforest.

ACTIVE / PASSIVE

2. The cricket ball was thrown by Phillip.

ACTIVE / PASSIVE

3. The principal examined students' school reports.

ACTIVE / PASSIVE

Question 5

Write your own sentences for the following **adverbs**.

a) Sadly

_____

b) Now

_____

c) Away

_____

d) Seldom

_____

ANSWERS TO VERBS AND ADVERBS

Question 1

SENTENCE	VERB	ADVERB	ADJECTIVE
It **was** my brother's birthday yesterday.	✓		
He was a **scrawny** boy.			✓
It was an **old-fashioned** looking room.			✓
She **wrote** a short story about grief.	✓		
The bees were **everywhere**.		✓	
She was too **young** to understand.			✓

Question 2

Adverbial phrases are phrases made up of two or more adverbs. For example the sentence 'she walked in as quietly as a mouse', is an adverbial phrase 'As quietly as a mouse' is the adverbial phrase, as it uses adverbs to modify the action.

Question 3

You could use any verbs so long as they describe the role of each profession Please get a parent or teacher to look at your answers.

<u>For example:</u>

a) Farmer = harvest, chop

b) Scientist = investigate, discover

c) Police Officer = protect, prevent

d) Nurse = care, write

Question 4

1. Active

2. Passive

3. Active

Question 5

*You could use any adverbs so long as they describe the role of each profession. Please get a parent or teacher to look at your answers.

<u>For example:</u>

a) Sadly, his grandmother passed away.

b) It was now time to head home.

c) Rachel turned away three customers.

d) We seldom see our cousins anymore.

HOW ARE YOU GETTING ON?

NOUNS
AND PRONOUNS

(Grammar)

NOUNS

NOUNS are <u>names of things.</u>

People

Animals

Places

Objects

Below are four *types* of nouns:

1. **PROPER NOUNS**
2. **COMMON NOUNS**
3. **COLLECTIVE NOUNS**
4. **ABSTRACT NOUNS**

PROPER
NOUNS

PROPER nouns are the names of <u>people</u> or <u>places</u> or <u>objects</u> or <u>days/months of the year</u>.

Germany (place)	Bedgebury Avenue (place)	River Thames (place)
Uppersfield United (teams)	**Friday** (day)	**April** (month)
Elizabeth (people)	**Ryan** (people)	**Harrison** (people)

NOUNS

COMMON NOUNS

COMMON nouns are words we use every day. They are **general, non-specific** words for <u>people</u>, <u>places</u> or <u>objects</u> or <u>things</u>.

gardens (place)	mountains (place)	house (place)
baby (people)	woman (people)	man (people)
fork (object)	chair (object)	penguin (animals)

Words that name something that you can see, taste, touch, smell or hear, are also known as **CONCRETE** nouns. Most nouns are concrete nouns and can either be proper or common nouns.

COLLECTIVE NOUNS

COLLECTIVE nouns are nouns that describe <u>groups</u> of things.

team (team of players)	crowd (crowd of people)	pack (pack of wolves)
swarm (swarm of bees)	flock (flock of birds)	herd (herd of sheep)

NOUNS

ABSTRACT nouns are words that describe things that you **cannot** <u>see</u>, <u>touch</u>, <u>taste</u>, <u>smell</u> or <u>hear</u>.

These words could describe particular <u>emotions</u> that someone might be feeling, and they could also describe <u>ideas</u>.

happiness	jealousy	anger
freedom	bravery	wisdom
love	hate	fear
curiosity	self-esteem	childhood

Names of countries, days of the week, months of the year, rivers, book titles, names of people and places to visit are ALL **PROPER** nouns and require CAPITAL LETTERS.

The main difference between **PROPER** nouns and **COMMON** nouns is as follows:

❖ A common noun names a general person, place or object;

❖ A proper noun names a specific person, place or object.

Remember, most nouns are **CONCRETE** nouns. Any word that describes something you can see, touch, taste, smell or hear is a **CONCRETE** noun. These can be **PROPER** or **COMMON** nouns.

PRONOUNS

PRONOUNS are used to <u>replace</u> nouns.

Pronouns help you to avoid repeating the same word over and over and *over* again.

We use pronouns **ALL** the time!

> See I've used 'WE' in this sentence to demonstrate pronouns.

1st PERSON PRONOUNS

I	Me	We	Us

2nd PERSON PRONOUNS

You

3rd PERSON PRONOUNS

He / Him	She / Her	They / Them	It

RELATIVE PRONOUNS

Who	That	Which	Where / When

POSSESSIVE PRONOUNS

Mine / Yours	Ours / Theirs	His / Hers	Its

POSSESSIVE pronouns NEVER use apostrophes.

Question 1

Colour all of the COLLECTIVE nouns in blue.

Colour all of the COMMON nouns in red.

Colour all of the PROPER nouns in yellow.

Colour all of the ABSTRACT nouns in green.

Swarm	Friendship	Ocean
Suit	T-Rex	Team
Fear	Titanic	Playground
Indian Ocean	Bunch	Jealousy
Chocolate	The Bible	Wealth

Question 2

Explain why the pronoun in the sentence should be changed to a proper noun instead.

Joey and Gareth went running but he got too tired, and so he had to stop.

_____

_____

Question 3

Circle whether to use the pronoun 'I' or 'me' in the following sentences.

a) My brother and _____ went on holiday (me,   I)

b) Is this really happening to _____? (me,   I)

c) Carrie and _____ love playing hockey. (I,   me)

Question 4

The following sentences do not use personal pronouns. Write out the sentences using a personal pronoun.

a) The car broke down along the motorway because the car ran out of fuel.

_____

b) Amelia was sent home from school. Amelia got into a fight with a girl in her class, Sarah. The teacher saw Amelia instigate the fight.

_____

_____

c) The snow fell heavy during the night and the snow caused chaos in the morning. The icy conditions meant that people couldn't get to work and the ice was causing disruptions to everyone's plans.

_____

_____

_____

Question 5

Using your answer to question 4 (part b), why do you think you should use Amelia's name as opposed to a personal pronoun in the sentence, 'the teacher saw Amelia instigate the fight'?

_____

_____

_____

Question 6

Underline all of the abstract nouns.

It was a brave decision for Tommy to make. He quickly made his way through the crashing waves and began swimming out to the woman, who was struggling to stay afloat. The truth was, Tommy was not a strong swimmer himself. After successfully rescuing the woman, Tommy felt that his courageous decision was an act of heroism.

ANSWERS TO NOUNS AND PRONOUNS

Question 1

Collective nouns (blue) = swarm, team, bunch

Common nouns (red) = ocean, suit, playground, chocolate

Proper nouns (yellow) = T-Rex, Titanic, Indian Ocean, The Bible

Abstract nouns (green) = friendship, fear, jealousy, wealth

Question 2

The sentence should read 'Joey and Gareth went running but Gareth (or Joey) got too tired, and so he had to stop'. Using a noun as opposed to a personal pronoun gives the sentence more clarity. With the pronoun 'he', we don't know who got tired, so a name would need to be used here, in order to determine who got too tired.

Question 3

a) My brother and **I** went on holiday

b) Is this really happening to **me**?

c) Carrie and **I** love playing hockey.

Question 4

a) The car broke down along the motorway, because **it** ran out of fuel.

b) Amelia was sent home from school. **She** got into a fight with a girl in her class, Sarah. The teacher saw Amelia instigate the fight.

c) The snow fell heavy during the night and **it** caused chaos in the morning. The icy conditions meant that people couldn't get to work and **it** was causing disruption to everyone's plans.

Question 5

The name 'Amelia' needs to be used in the sentence 'the teacher saw Amelia instigate the fight', because a personal pronoun would make it unclear as to who started the fight – Amelia or Sarah. Therefore, a name needs to be given in order to clarify who.

Question 6

It was a brave decision for Tommy to make. He quickly made his way through the crashing waves and began swimming out to the woman who was struggling to stay afloat. The <u>truth</u> was, Tommy was not a strong swimmer himself. After successfully rescuing the woman, Tommy felt that his courageous decision was an act of <u>heroism</u>.

THE
REVISION
SERIES

TENSES

(Grammar)

TENSES

VERBS AND THEIR CORRECT TENSE

When it comes to writing any piece of text, it is important that you are able to use the correct verb form, to indicate whether something is happening, has happened, or will happen.

This is known as using the correct verb tense.

There are three tenses that you need to be aware of:

Past

- The past tense indicates something that has already happened, or used to happen.
- It can be used to describe something that has just happened.

Present

- The present tense indicates something happening at this very moment.
- It can also be used to describe something that happens regularly.

Future

- The future tense indicates something that is going to happen in the future.

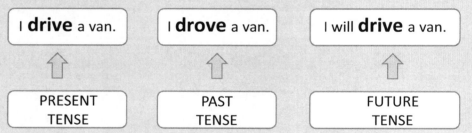

| I **drive** a van. | I **drove** a van. | I will **drive** a van. |

| ⇧ | ⇧ | ⇧ |

| PRESENT TENSE | PAST TENSE | FUTURE TENSE |

THE CONDITIONAL TENSE

The conditional tense is a tense used to describe something that could, would, might or should happen.

I **should** finish my homework.

I **might** go to the cinema after work.

TENSES

VARIATIONS OF TENSES

Now that you know what the three tenses are, you should also know that there are some variations of these tenses.

PAST	
SIMPLE PAST	I **did** my school project.
PAST CONTINUOUS	I **was doing** my school project.
PERFECT TENSE	I **have done** my school project.
PAST PERFECT	I **had done** my school project.
PRESENT	
SIMPLE PRESENT	I **walk** outside.
PRESENT CONTINUOUS	I **am walking** outside.
FUTURE	
SIMPLE FUTURE	She **will be** nervous.
FUTURE PERFECT	She **will have been** nervous the first day of school.

PAST TENSE is something that has already happened, or used to happen.

PRESENT TENSE is something that is currently happening or happens regularly.

FUTURE TENSE is something that is going to happen.

CONDITIONAL TENSE is something that might, could or should happen.

Question 1

Give a definition of the following tenses, along with two example sentences.

PAST TENSE

_____

_____

EXAMPLE 1

_____

EXAMPLE 2

_____

PRESENT TENSE

_____

_____

EXAMPLE 1

_____

EXAMPLE 2

_____

FUTURE TENSE

_____

_____

EXAMPLE 1

_____

EXAMPLE 2

_____

CONDITIONAL TENSE

EXAMPLE 1

EXAMPLE 2

Question 2

Fill in the blank spaces in the table below. <u>The first row has been completed for you</u>.

SIMPLE PAST	PAST PARTICIPLE	PRESENT
Chose	Have chosen	Choose
		Lose
Grew		
	Have had	
		Forget
Flown		

Question 3

Circle the two words that are in the correct tense, in order for the sentences to read correctly.

a) The celebrity _____ hundreds of autographs and then _____ to call it a day.

   DECIDE   **SIGN**   **SIGNED**   **DECIDES**   **DECIDED**

b) Abbie's mum told her if she _____ her homework, she _____ be able to watch some TV before bed.

   FINISH   **WILL**   **WILL HAVE**   **WOULD**   **FINISHED**

c) The runner _____ to catch up with her opponent but she couldn't. However, the runner _____ beat her personal best.

   TRY   **TRIED**   **DO**   **DOES**   **DID**

ANSWERS TO TENSES

Question 1

Past

The past tense indicates something that has already happened, or used to happen.

You could come up with any two examples, so long as you have used the past tense correctly. Get a parent or teacher to check your examples.

Present

The present tense indicates something happening at this very moment.

You could come up with any two examples, so long as you have used the present tense correctly. Get a parent or teacher to check your examples.

Future

The future tense indicates something is going to happen in the future.

You could come up with any two examples, so long as you have used the future tense correctly. Get a parent or teacher to check your examples.

Conditional tense

The conditional tense is a tense used to describe something that could, would, might or should happen.

You could come up with any two examples, so long as you have used the conditional tense correctly. Get a parent or teacher to check your examples.

Question 2

SIMPLE PAST	PAST PARTICIPLE	PRESENT
Chose	Have chosen	Choose
Lost	Have lost	Lose
Grew	Have grown	Grow
Had	Have had	Have
Forgot	Have forgotten	Forget
Flown	Have flown	Fly

Question 3

a) The celebrity _____ hundreds of autographs and then
_____ to call it a day.

    DECIDE   **SIGN**   **(SIGNED)**   **DECIDES**   **(DECIDED)**

b) Abbie's mum told her if she _____ her homework, she
_____ be able to watch some TV before bed.

    FINISH   **WILL**   **WILL HAVE**   **(WOULD)**   **(FINISHED)**

c) The runner _____ to catch up with her opponent but she couldn't.
However, the runner _____ beat her personal best.

    TRY   **(TRIED)**   **DO**   **DOES**   **(DID)**

HOW ARE YOU GETTING ON?

THE
REVISION
SERIES

BEGINNING AND ENDING SENTENCES

(Punctuation)

CAPITAL LETTERS

CAPITAL LETTERS are a great way to <u>break up</u> the text and make it visually clearer.

There are two main reasons to use CAPITAL LETTERS:

1. Capital letters are used to begin new sentences.
2. Certain words will always begin with a capital letter.

CAPITAL LETTERS ARE USED TO BEGIN NEW SENTENCES

ALL sentences NEED to begin with a capital letter.

> **E**very sentence needs to begin with a capital letter

- When a full stop is used, the next word will begin with a capital letter.

CERTAIN WORDS WILL ALWAYS BEGIN WITH A CAPITAL LETTER

Even in the middle of a sentence, some words will ALWAYS begin with a capital letter.

Proper nouns ALWAYS begin with a capital letter. These include:

People's names	People's titles	Names of businesses	Titles of films, books, plays, programmes
Countries and nationalities	Days and months	Towns and cities	The word 'I'

Some words are tricky. Sometimes, words will be capitalised, and sometimes they won't be.

For example:

I live in the solar system, on Earth.

- If you are talking about something specific, you would capitalise the word.

The earth around us was damp and soggy.

- If you are talking about something in generic terms, you would not capitalise the word.

FULL STOPS

FULL STOPS are used to show the end of a sentence.

> See how this full stop marks the end of the sentence.

Full stops are used to end sentences that are telling you something.

Without full stops, it would be really difficult to read large amounts of information. Sentences would run in to one another, and therefore make it confusing.

Some sentences may not end with a full stop. You might decide to use an ellipsis, or exclamation or question mark. These will be discussed further on in the book, so keep an eye out!

Use a full stop to finish a sentence.

ELLIPSIS

Ellipsis are another punctuation mark that you could use to end a sentence.

An ellipsis looks like this: ...

This should only be used to add suspense or leave a sentence intentionally unfinished.

> He walked into the dark, empty room, and suddenly...

> "I'm sorry. I thought I had..."

QUESTION MARKS

QUESTION MARKS are used to end sentences that are a question.

ALL questions will need a question mark to end the sentence.

IDENTIFYING QUESTIONS

You can usually tell a question is being asked, if the sentence starts with the following words:

What do you want for dinner?

When do you want me to come round?

Why are you here?

Some questions might not start with the above words.

Does the sentence read as though someone is asking something?

Do you want to come round after school?

I am hungry, aren't you?

Is it lunchtime yet?

QUESTION MARKS

BE CAREFUL!

Sometimes a sentence looks like it is asking a question, but it's ACTUALLY NOT.

<u>Take a look at the below example:</u>

Harry asked, "What do you want to eat?"	**QUESTION**
Harry asked me what I want to eat.	**NOT A QUESTION**

Some questions look like a question, but they don't actually ask one!

- In the above example:

  Harry asked me what I want to eat – although this tells you about a question and *looks* like a question, it is NOT actually asking the question. Therefore you would not put a question mark here.

QUESTION MARK PROMPTS

WHO   WHERE   WHY   HOW   WHAT   WHEN   WHICH

Watch out for sentences that LOOK like a question, but do NOT actually ask anything.

EXCLAMATION MARKS

EXCLAMATION MARKS are very tricky to use and you must use them correctly! These are another way you can end a sentence.

Exclamation marks can be used instead of a full stop to end sentences.

These should ONLY be used to show really, really, really strong feelings.

WHEN TO USE EXCLAMATION MARKS

WHEN TO USE EXCLAMATION MARKS
• Indicate strong emotions • Indicate a command • Indicate anger, surprise or suspense • Indicate someone shouting or raised voices

Exclamation marks can be used in short, snappy sentences.

Ouch!	"Fire!" she screamed.	Bang!	How amazing!

You can use exclamation marks to show a **COMMAND**. This should only be done if the command is URGENT or IMPORTANT.

Stop it!	Shut the window!	Sit still!	Help me!

DO NOT use exclamation marks in formal writing.

NEVER use more than one exclamation mark!

Question 1

Explain why we use exclamation marks.

_____

_____

Question 2

Explain why we use question marks.

_____

_____

Question 3

Put a tick or cross in the boxes to indicate whether the following sentence is punctuated correctly.

SENTENCE	IS IT CORRECT?
The queen is appearing at the garden party.	
Are you going on holiday this year!	
My grandmother is French, and she is trying to teach me the French language.	
That was immense!	
Are you ready for your exam?	
It was important that i did well in my last test.	
Sally was born in October. Her birthday was the day before halloween.	

Question 4

Explain the use of an ellipsis.

_____

_____

Question 5

Circle whether you think the sentence is a direct question or indirect question
Draw in the question mark if the sentence is a question.

a) Charlie asked where his dinosaur was   DIRECT / INDIRECT

b) Are you hungry   DIRECT / INDIRECT

c) I wondered what time dinner would be   DIRECT / INDIRECT

d) Aren't you tired yet   DIRECT / INDIRECT

e) It's funny, don't you think   DIRECT / INDIRECT

Question 6

Rewrite the following sentences, correcting any missing or wrongly placed
capital letters and full stops.

1. the chinese government implemented a policy in the late 1970's to
    address and reduce the country's birth rate they decided to introduce
    a one-child policy to create benefits such as access to education and
    better healthcare.

    _____

    _____

    _____

2. henry viii was king of england and had six wives he was born in 1491,
    which in english History, is known as the tudor age. The term "tudor"
    originated from henry viii, whose family name was 'tudor'

    _____

    _____

    _____

3. for new year's eve, katie and andy spent the day in london at hyde park they walked around london and went ice skating "it was one of the best days of my life", proclaimed katie, who loved spending the day with her boyfriend

_____

_____

_____

Question 7

For the following statements, circle true if the statement is correct, and false if it is incorrect.

a) Capital letters will need to be used for all nouns.

TRUE / FALSE

b) The names of people will always begin with a capital letter.

TRUE / FALSE

c) An ellipsis is used as a way of finishing a sentence abruptly.

TRUE / FALSE

d) A question mark will be needed for indirect questions.

TRUE / FALSE

e) The word 'king' can be written with a capital letter and without.

TRUE / FALSE

ANSWERS TO BEGINNING AND ENDING SENTENCES

Question 1

Exclamation marks are used to highlight strong feelings or commands.

Question 2

Question marks are used to show that someone has asked a question.

Question 3

SENTENCE	IS IT CORRECT?
The queen is appearing at the garden party.	✘
Are you going on holiday this year!	✘
My grandmother is French, and she is trying to teach me the French language.	✔
That was immense!	✔
Are you ready for your exam?	✔
It was important that i did well in my last test.	✘
Sally was born in October. Her birthday was the day before halloween.	✘

Question 4

Ellipses are a way of ending a sentence which adds suspense or leaves the sentence intentionally unfinished.

Question 5

a) Charlie asked where his dinosaur was

INDIRECT

b) Are you hungry?

DIRECT

c) I wondered what time dinner would be

INDIRECT

d) Aren't you tired yet?

DIRECT

e) It's funny, don't you think?

DIRECT

Question 6

1. The Chinese Government implemented a policy in the late 1970's to address and reduce the country's birth rate. They decided to introduce a one-child policy to create benefits such as access to education and better healthcare.

2. Henry VIII was King of England and had six wives. He was born in 1491, which in English history, is known as the Tudor Age. The term "Tudor" originated from Henry VIII, whose family name was 'Tudor'.

3. For New Year's Eve, Katie and Andy spent the day in London at Hyde Park. They walked around London and went ice skating. "It was one of the best days of my life," proclaimed Katie, who loved spending the day with her boyfriend.

Question 7

a) Capital letters will need to be used for all nouns.

FALSE

b) The names of people will always begin with a capital letter.

TRUE

c) An ellipsis is used as a way of finishing a sentence abruptly.

FALSE

d) A question mark will be needed for indirect questions.

FALSE

e) The word 'king' can be written with a capital letter and without.

TRUE

HOW ARE YOU GETTING ON?

THE
REVISION
SERIES

COMMAS AND INVERTED COMMAS

(Punctuation)

COMMAS

COMMAS are a great way to make your writing easier to read.

You should remember to use commas when writing lists, or break up long sentences.

USE COMMAS WHEN WRITING LISTS

There are a few points you need to remember when using commas in lists:

1. A comma needs to be placed after every item in your list, **apart from the last two**.
2. In order to separate the last two items in your list, you should use **"and"** or **"or"**.
3. If the last two items in the list already use the word "and", you will need to place a **comma** and an **"and"** before that item.

> Harrison's best friends were Matt, James, Sam and Lionel.

> The girl stood tall, slim and elegantly.

> At the restaurant, we ordered pie and chips, fish and chips, and a raspberry cheesecake.

> If the last two words use 'and', this will need to be separated from the rest of the items, but still read as one.
> For example: 'We ordered pie and chips, fish and chips, and a raspberry cheesecake' – this shows that the fish and chips come together, and is separated from other items such as pie and chips.

COMMAS

COMMAS CAN BE USED TO BREAK UP LONG SENTENCES

Commas can be used to break up clauses in order to break up the compound sentence and make it easier to read.

You need to avoid your reader getting confused. Commas will help you to break up sentences, when more than one thing is happening or being spoken about.

Sometimes in a sentence, extra information is added to make the sentence more interesting. A comma can be used to separate that extra information from the main clause.

> Teresa stopped in her tracks, she was unsure which direction to go.

> Despite being told off, I continued to misbehave.

> Bob's fireplace, which has been there since he moved in, is starting to fall apart.

> Can you see, in the last example, there are two commas positioned in the sentence. The middle part of the sentence, "which has been there since he moved in" is an embedded clause. This provides us with EXTRA information. The overall clause is that Bob's fireplace is falling apart.

ADDING EXTRA INFORMATION

As shown in the last example, a pair of commas are used. This is to break off the middle part of the sentence – which on its own, doesn't make sense.

> Bob's fireplace, *which has been there since he moved in,* is starting to fall apart.

- Bob's fireplace is falling apart – this is the main clause.
- Bob's fireplace, which has been there since he moved in– this is EXTRA information.

INVERTED COMMAS

INVERTED COMMAS are also known as **SPEECH MARKS**.

"   **"**

speech

Speech marks are used to highlight when someone is talking.

There are a few rules that you need to remember when using inverted commas:

Rule 1

Use inverted commas only around the words that are ACTUALLY SPOKEN. You should NOT use speech marks if you are quoting reported speech (they are not the ACTUAL words that were spoken).

Rule 2

A CAPITAL LETTER should be used on the first word that is spoken.

Rule 3

If a sentence goes into speech, a comma will need to be placed before the speech starts.

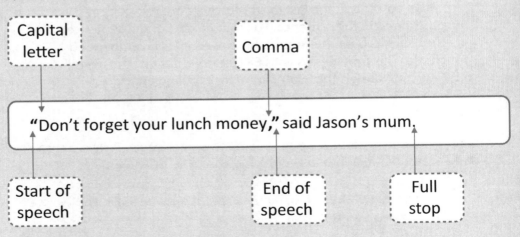

INVERTED COMMAS

Rule 4

If the sentence ends with the speech, a full stop should be placed inside the closing inverted comma.

Rule 5

If the sentence continues after the speech, a comma should be placed inside the closing inverted comma.

Rule 6

If more than one person is speaking, you should write their speeches on different lines.

DIRECT SPEECH = exact words that someone says.

> Michael said, "It's too cold for ice cream."

REPORTED SPEECH = are words that someone has said, but you have written in your own words.

> Michael said that it was too cold for ice cream.

REPORTED SPEECH = not the EXACT words!

COMMAS should be used to indicate items in a list.

You can check to see if you have used the commas in the correct place, by replacing them with 'and' or 'or' and seeing whether the sentence makes sense.

INVERTED COMMAS should ONLY be used for DIRECT SPEECH. REPORTED SPEECH DOES NOT require inverted commas (speech marks).

Question 1

Tick the boxes if the sentence is punctuated correctly.

a) I like playing football, hockey and tennis.

b) "What is the time, said Pete".

c) However, I did not expect that.

d) My teacher, Miss Day, was the best English teacher at school.

e) Even though I was unprepared, I passed with flying colours.

Question 2

The following sentences need commas in order to make the structure of the sentence less ambiguous. Draw the comma in the correct place for each sentence. More than one comma may be needed.

a) "Let's go out and play" Sarah said excitedly.

b) My favourite foods are pasta burgers lasagne and beef stew and dumplings.

c) Neil a children's doctor wants to take a holiday.

d) "Hurry up" exclaimed Johnny who was waiting impatiently for his friend.

Question 3

Give two reasons as to when you would use a comma.

_____

_____

_____

_____

Question 4

Explain how the **commas** change the meaning of both sentences below:

Mountain gorillas, which live in Africa, are endangered animals.

Mountain gorillas which live in Africa are endangered animals.

_____

_____

_____

_____

Question 5

The following sentences need commas in order to make the sentences read coherently. Draw the **comma** in the correct place for each sentence. <u>More than one comma may be needed.</u>

a) Suddenly we heard a loud knock at the door.

b) Vinnie's mum had blown up blue green red and orange balloons.

c) Freddie a frightened young boy was scared to go to school.

d) "Listen up" shouted the teacher. She was getting very impatient with one student in particular.

Question 6

What is the difference between direct speech and indirect speech? Give an example of direct speech and indirect speech.

_____

_____

EXAMPLE 1

_____

EXAMPLE 2

_____

ANSWERS TO COMMAS AND INVERTED COMMAS

Question 1

The boxes you should have ticked were a, c, d and e.

Question 2

a) "Let's go out and play," Sarah said, excitedly.

b) My favourite foods are pasta, burgers, lasagne, and beef stew and dumplings.

c) Neil, a children's doctor, wants to take a holiday.

d) "Hurry up," exclaimed Johnny, who was waiting impatiently for his friend.

Question 3

Commas need to be used to demonstrate a list format. For example, "I went to the park and played on the swings, the slide, the roundabout and the climbing frame." This separates each item in the list. Commas are also used to allow you to add in extra information. For example, "The dog, which was fluffy and white, had to go to the vet." This shows two sets of information which have been separated with the use of commas.

Question 4

The first sentence uses the commas to separate the 'which live in Africa'. This sentence is implying that all mountain gorillas live in Africa. The second sentence implies that only the mountain gorillas in Africa are endangered.

Question 5

a) Suddenly, we heard a loud knock at the door.

b) Vinnie's mum had blown up blue, green, red and orange balloons.

c) Freddie, a frightened young boy, was scared to go to school.

d) "Listen up," shouted the teacher. She was getting very impatient, with one student in particular.

Question 6

Direct speech is when someone is directly asking a question, whereas an indirect question is a statement that sounds like a question, but no question is actually being asked.

EXAMPLE 1

"What time do you get home from work?" – Direct question.

EXAMPLE 2

Sammie asked her mum what time she would be home from work. – Indirect question.

HOW ARE YOU GETTING ON?

APOSTROPHES

(Punctuation)

APOSTROPHES

APOSTROPHES are used for two main reasons: to show possession and to join two words to make one.

SINGULAR POSSESSIONS

One of the reasons you will need to use apostrophes is to show possession. The apostrophe is used to show that one thing belongs to another.

You will need to add an apostrophe and an 's' to show that it belongs to someone.

Rachel**'s** shoes.

The cat**'s** food.

The girl**'s** chair.

- The shoes belong to Rachel.
- The food belongs to the cat.
- The chair belongs to the girl.

This also applies to words ending in 's'.

James**'s** hair is black.

The octopus**'s** head.

It was Dickens**'s** novel.

APOSTROPHES

PLURAL POSSESSIONS
If something belongs to a group of people or things, a different rule applies.

Rule 1
If the word is plural and ends in an 's', you just need to add an apostrophe.

Neighbours'	Babies'	Cats'	Dogs'

Rule 2
If the word is plural, and doesn't end in an 's', you need to add an apostrophe and an 's'.

Men's	Women's	Children's

ITS versus IT'S

It is important that you know the difference between **ITS** and **IT'S**.

ITS ⟹ indicates possession.

The dog ate its bone.	The bird went on its way.

- This is like saying 'his' or 'hers'.
- Although it sounds the same as 'it's', it needs to be used in a completely different context.
- 'Its' should be used to show that something belongs to someone or something.

APOSTROPHES

IT'S ➡️ a contraction for 'it is' or 'it has'.

| It's snowing. | It's started to rain. |

- It's basically means *'it is'* or *'it has'*.
- The apostrophe shows us that a letter has been removed in order to combine the two words.
- For the above examples:
  - o   It is snowing.
  - o   It has started to rain.
- **IT'S** should NEVER be used to show possession. If it belongs to someone or something, than you would use **ITS**. If it is a contraction of *'it is'* or *'it has'*, then you need to use **IT'S**.

SINGULAR POSSESSIONS – Add an apostrophe and an 's' (to show that it belongs to someone or something). This is also the same for singular words ending in 's'.

PLURAL POSSESSIONS – If it ends in an 's', just add an apostrophe. If it doesn't end in an 's', add an apostrophe and an 's'.

ITS – shows possession. Belonging to someone (his or hers).

IT'S – a contraction of the words 'it is' or 'it has'.

APOSTROPHES

CONTRACTIONS USE APOSTROPHES

Apostrophes are also used to join two words together.

Apostrophes show that you have omitted or left out some of the letters, in order to join two words.

Below is a list of the common type of contracted words. LEARN as many of them as you can.

It's (It is)	I'm (I am)	I've (I have)	Don't (Do not)	Who's (Who is)
Doesn't (Does not)	I'll (I will)	Let's (Let us)	Won't (Will not)	Can't (Cannot)
He's (He is)	She's (She is)	They're (They are)	They'll (They will)	Hasn't (Has not)
I'd (I would)	We'd (We would)	Would've (Would have)	We're (We are)	Haven't (Have not)

Can you think of any other contacted words?

REMEMBER = apostrophes
are used to show possession
and omission!

Question 1

Explain the difference between **ITS** and **IT'S**, using examples to support you answer.

_____

_____

_____

_____

Question 2

Explain the difference between LETS and LET'S, using examples to suppor your answer.

_____

_____

_____

_____

Question 3

Below are three statements about using apostrophes. Circle whether the statement is true or false.

a) If you use the word **ITS**, that means it is showing that something belongs to someone or something.

TRUE / FALSE

b) A word for a group of people ending in 's', will need just an apostrophe when showing that something belongs to someone or something.

TRUE / FALSE

c) The following sentence should not have an apostrophe: "Let's have some fun."

TRUE / FALSE

Question 4

Rewrite the following sentences so that each sentence contains a possessive apostrophe.

a) The shorts that belonged to Adam fell down when he came off the slide.

_____

_____

b) The horse that belongs to Sandra was young and energetic.

_____

_____

c) The car that belonged to Dave and his wife had been stolen.

_____

_____

Question 5

For the following words, write out their contracted word and then use the contraction in a sentence.

a) Was not = _____

_____

b) Might have = _____

_____

c) She will = _____

_____

ANSWERS TO APOSTROPHES

Question 1

ITS is a word that should be used to show possession. It takes the place of words like hers or his. For example, 'London is well known for its tourist attractions'. Whereas, the word IT'S is a contraction of the words 'it is' or 'it has'. For example, 'it's really hot today' can be replaced with 'it is really hot today'.

Question 2

LETS is a word that should be used to mean 'allow'. This doesn't require an apostrophe. For example, 'Rachel lets her sister play with her make up.' Whereas, the word LET'S is a contraction of the words 'let us'. For example, 'Let's go outside', could also be written as, 'Let us go outside'.

Question 3

a) If you use the word **ITS**, that means it is showing that something be-longs to someone or something.

   TRUE = Its is a way of showing possession, whereas the word 'it's' is used for 'it is' or 'it has'.

b) A word for a group of people ending in 's', will need just an apostrophe when showing that something belongs to someone or something.

   TRUE = a group of people that ends in an 's' such as babies or neigh-bours, only needs an apostrophe when showing that something belongs to someone or something.

c) The following sentence should not have an apostrophe: "Let's have some fun."

   FALSE = the word 'let's' is a contraction of 'let us'.

Question 4

a) Adam's shorts fell down when he came off the slide.

b) Sandra's horse was young and energetic.

c) Dave and his wife's car had been stolen.

Question 5

For this question, you could have used any sentence, so long as you have used the contraction correctly.

<u>For example:</u>

a) Wasn't

It wasn't my fault.

b) Might've

I might've been late for school.

c) She'll

She'll be back.

HOW ARE YOU GETTING ON?

THE
REVISION
SERIES

COLONS AND SEMI-COLONS

(Punctuation)

COLONS

COLONS are another punctuation mark that you will need to learn. This punctuation mark consists of two dots, one above the other.

■

■

They are a great way to introduce new information in **list format**.

LIST FORMATS

If you are introducing a list, you can use a colon to break up the sentence, using a list format.

> The following ingredients are needed to make chocolate brownies: 400g caster sugar, 225g of melted butter, 60g cocoa powder, 4 eggs, 1 tablespoon vanilla extract, 225g plain flour, ½ teaspoon baking powder and ½ teaspoon salt.

- A colon should ONLY be used if it follows the main clause of the sentence.
- For example, if the above passage, started with "I need…" this would not need a colon because "I need" is not a main clause. (See the main clause section for more information).

As well as list formats, you can also position a colon before you write a list of bullet points:

> The following ingredients are needed to make chocolate brownies:
> - 400g caster sugar
> - 225g of melted butter
> - 60g cocoa powder
> - 4 eggs
> - 1 tablespoon vanilla extract
> - 225g plain flour
> - ½ teaspoon baking powder
> - ½ teaspoon salt.

COLONS

INTRODUCING EXPLANATIONS

Colons can also be used in sentences to break up the sentence. They work similarly to a comma, but the two sentences have to be about the <u>same thing</u>.

> Mikey has a dilemma: he can't remember where he put his homework.

> Some people love football : other people can't stand it.

- The first part of the sentence needs to make sense as a standalone sentence.
- The second part after the colon provides more information about the first part.

COLONS are often used in list formats.

COLONS can also be used to provide further information about the initial clause being made.

SEMI-COLONS

You need to be able to know the difference between **colons** and **semi-colons**.

SEMI-COLONS consist of one full stop, positioned above a comma.

There are two main reasons to use a semi-colon:
1. Break up longer lists.
2. Break up two closely related main clauses.

BREAK UP LONGER LISTS

Like colons, semi-colons can be used to break up lists. However, you would use a semi-colon if the list consisted of longer sentences.

You will need to put a semi-colon before the 'and' or 'or', which joins the last two things on the list.

> If you go to the shop, can you get me half a dozen eggs; a
> pint of milk; three loaves of bread; a chocolate bar; and a box
> of tea bags.

BREAK UP TWO CLOSELY RELATED MAIN CLAUSES

You can also join two sentences together with the use of semi-colons.

These two sentences will talk about the same subject and will be equally important.

You could separate the two sentences with a full stop and they would both still make sense.

> Ollie was really tired; Marcus wanted to play.

> James played football at break time; Daniel played rugby.

Question 1

Give a definition of a colon and come up with three example sentences.

Colon

_____

_____

_____

Example 1

_____

_____

Example 2

_____

_____

Example 3

_____

_____

Question 2

Give a definition of a semi-colon and come up with three example sentences

Semi-colon

_____

_____

_____

Example 1

_____

_____

Example 2

_____

_____

Example 3

_____

_____

Question 3

For the following sentences, insert a semi-colon or colon in the correct places
More than one punctuation mark may be required.

a) We went to the grocery store and we bought mushrooms, onions, toma-toes, and pasta.

b) The teacher was impressed I scored top marks on a pop quiz.

c) When I'm older, I want to go travelling become a professional football player and start a family.

d) Giraffes have long necks they use them to reach their food.

e) This is my to-do list hoover, put the dishwasher on, iron the clothes and pick up the kids from school.

ANSWERS TO COLONS AND SEMI-COLONS

Question 1

Colon

Colons are used to illustrate list formats. They can also be used to expand sentences and provide further details.

Example 1 – I was nervous: I hated meeting new people.

Example 2 - My grandma gave me a list of groceries to get at the shop: milk, teabags, sugar and cookies.

Example 3 – There is only one thing I want to do today: go to the park.

Question 2

Semi-colon

Semi-colons are used to either break up long clauses or break up lists which include long phrases.

Example 1 – Harry is a dentist; Martin is a decorator.

Example 2 – We played snooker; had some food; and went out dancing.

Example 3 – Linda is a vegetarian; Jamie is vegan.

Question 3

a) We went to the grocery store and we bought: mushrooms, onions, tomatoes, and pasta.

b) The teacher was impressed; I scored top marks on a pop quiz.

c) When I'm older, I want to go travelling; become a professional football player; and start a family.

d) Giraffes have long necks: they use them to reach their food.

e) This is my to-do list: hoover, put the dishwasher on, iron the clothes and pick up the kids from school.

HOW ARE YOU GETTING ON?

THE
REVISION
SERIES

BRACKETS, DASHES AND HYPHENS

(Punctuation)

BRACKETS

BRACKETS are used to separate any added information.

(*EXTRA information* **)**

They are a great way to keep EXTRA *bits* of information together.

> Trevor (the King of frogs) sat on his big, green leaf.

If you removed the brackets, the rest of the sentence would still make sense.

DASHES

DASHES are very similar to brackets.

A **pair of dashes** can be used in the exact same context as brackets.

> Drake - the Managing Director - was away on holiday for three weeks.

If you removed the pair of dashes, the rest of the sentence would still make sense.

A **single dash** can be used to emphasise a <u>pause</u> in the middle of the sentence. This pause is usually for dramatic effect.

> I climbed to the top of the mountain - it was exhausting!

HYPHENS

HYPHENS are used to join words together.

For example:
- Semi-final
- Co-own (sometimes, if the two words begin with the same letter, a hyphen is needed to make the word easier to read.)

Hyphens are also used to join words that should be read together.

For example:
- Flesh-eating
- Father-in-law
- Twenty-three

BRACKETS – Use brackets to separate information. Generally, if you removed the information within the brackets, the sentence would still make sense.

DASHES – Dashes can be used instead of brackets; they are both very similar. Insert two dashes (one before and one after the added bit of information). Again, if you removed the information within the dashes, the sentence would still make sense.

HYPHENS – join two closely related or parts of words together.

Question 1

Give an explanation of why you would use a single dash, using two example sentences to support your answer.

_____

_____

_____

EXAMPLE 1

_____

EXAMPLE 2

_____

Question 2

Give an explanation of why you would use pairs of dashes, using two example sentences to support your answer.

_____

_____

_____

EXAMPLE 1

_____

EXAMPLE 2

_____

Question 3

Give an explanation of why you would use brackets, using two example sentences to support your answer.

_____
_____
_____

EXAMPLE 1

_____

EXAMPLE 2

_____

Question 4

Look at the sentences, and write a brief exclamation of how the hyphen changes the meaning of the sentence.

a) A woman eating octopus.

A woman-eating octopus.

_____
_____

b) Thirty-odd strangers.

Thirty odd strangers.

_____

_____

ANSWERS TO BRACKETS, DASHES AND HYPHENS

Question 1

Single dashes can be used to provide a dramatic pause in a sentence.

Example 1: We thought the room was empty – until we heard a loud bang.

Example 2: It was quiet – too quiet.

(PLEASE NOTE: you could have written any sentence, so long as you have used the dash correctly. Get a parent or teacher to check that your sentences are correct).

Question 2

Pairs of dashes can be used in the same way as you would use brackets; to include extra information.

Example 1: My cats – Sally and Fluffy – are very playful.

Example 2: The builder – a tall, muscular man – had spent 9 hours working in the hot sun.

(PLEASE NOTE: you could have written any sentence, so long as you have used the pairs of dashes correctly.)

Question 3

Brackets can be used in order to separate information.

Example 1: As we arrived at the premiere (of my boyfriend's new film), the paparazzi were already and waiting.

Example 2: Polly (a quiet and talented, young girl) was applying for a music scholarship.

(PLEASE NOTE: you could have written any sentence, so long as you have used the brackets correctly.)

Question 4

a) A woman eating octopus suggests the woman is eating the octopus, whereas a woman-eating octopus suggests that the octopus eats women.

b) Thirty-odd strangers suggests an approximation, whereas thirty odd strangers suggests thirty peculiar strangers.

HOW ARE YOU GETTING ON?

THE
REVISION
SERIES

IMPROVE
YOUR SPELLING

(Spelling)

IMPROVING YOUR SPELLING

There are so many different rules about words and spellings, it makes it difficult to know whether or not you are writing them correctly – especially when lots of these words BREAK those rules!

LONG AND SHORT VOWELS

Vowels sound different depending on the word that it is in.

- Short vowels are snappy and quick.
- Long vowels are stretched out.

<u>For example:</u>

'A' is a short vowel. However, this vowel can also be stretched out to sound like 'ay'.

THE MAGIC 'E'

You can change the way a vowel sounds by adding an 'e' to the end of the word.

FAT	=	FATE
BATH	=	BATHE

If the word has a long vowel sound, this usually has an 'E' at the end of the word.

HOWEVER, there are some exceptions to this rule!

IMPROVING YOUR SPELLING

THE 'I' BEFORE 'E' EXCEPT AFTER 'C' RULE

A lot of words contain two vowels next to one another.

There is a very special rule if the two vowels next to one another are 'I' and 'E'.

I BEFORE E

Bel**ie**ve   fr**ie**nd   rel**ie**ve   tr**ie**s   pr**ie**st   th**ie**f

AFTER C

C**ei**ling   rec**ei**ve   perc**ei**ve   dec**ei**ve   conc**ei**ted

SOUNDS LIKE 'AY'

Sl**ei**gh   n**ei**ghbour   v**ei**n   fr**ei**ght   w**ei**ght

EXCEPTIONS!

L**ei**sure   for**ei**gn   **ei**ther   anc**ie**nt   w**ei**rd   s**ei**ze

However, this rule is not to be taken definitively. There are quite a few words that are an exception to this rule, and therefore schools have stopped focusing on this rule as it's not completely accurate. We have included this as a demonstration of how words are often perceived, and to provide a general overview of words with 'IE' and 'EI'.

IMPROVING YOUR SPELLING

SILENT LETTERS

This is a nasty one and can catch you out!

Some letters are written in words but are not actually spoken when you read that word out loud.

Below are some examples of words that contain silent letters.

SILENT W	SILENT G	SILENT K
Wrist Wrong Write Answer Two Whole	Design Foreign Gnome Night Campaign Sign	Knight Knee Know Knife Knit Knowledge
SILENT B	**SILENT H**	**SILENT N**
Thumb Lamb Doubt Climb Plumber Numb	White When Rhythm Hour Ghost Why	Autumn Column Solemn Hymn Condemn Damn
SILENT L	**SILENT T**	**SILENT U**
Palm Should Talk Balm Salmon Chalk	Witch Listen Mortgage Watch Castle Kitchen	Biscuit Tongue Guess Guitar Build Guy

UNSTRESSED LETTERS

Sometimes, vowels sound like <u>different</u> vowels.

Other times, some vowels cannot be heard.

| War | Wor | = the vowel 'a' sounds like an 'o'. |

| Interesting | Intresting | = the vowel 'e' is often unheard in this word. |

IMPROVING YOUR SPELLING

COMMONLY MISSPELT WORDS

There are lots of words in the English language that are commonly misspelt. The most commonly misspelt words are words that can be written as one or two words – each of which have completely different meanings.

Below I have broken down some of the most common words that are spelt incorrectly, or used in the wrong context.

Anybody Any body	Maybe May be	Anyway Any way	No one Nobody
Into In to	A lot	Thank you	In fact

Can you see how some words can be written in two different ways? These words would be used in completely different contexts. That is why it is important that you know when to use the correct spelling.

<u>For example:</u>

- Any body – is talking about a physical body.
  Anybody – is talking about anyone.

- May be – is talking about what might happen.
  Maybe – is talking about 'perhaps'.

- Into – is talking about when something moves towards the inside.
  In to – would be used for times when you are describing something as going into something.

- The words 'thank you,' 'a lot' and 'in fact' are always written as two words. It is never correct to write these words as one.

Can you think of any other words that you might be spelling incorrectly?

IMPROVING YOUR SPELLING

UNDERSTANDING WORDS

Some words are quite tricky when it comes to knowing which one to use.

<u>For example:</u>

Do you know when you should use the words 'who,' 'whom' and 'whose'?

> **WHO –** if the thing you're talking about is the subject, i.e. doing the action - use WHO.

> **WHOM –** if the thing you're talking about is the object, i.e. having the action done to it - use WHOM.

> **WHO'S –** this basically means "who is" or "who has".

> **WHOSE –** this is possessive; a way of saying who it belongs to.

Do you know when you should use the word 'who,' 'which' and 'that'?

> **WHO –** use the word 'who' for people.

> **WHICH –** when you're talking about things or animals.

> **THAT –** this can refer to things or animals, but you should try to use 'who' or 'which' where possible.

The best way to improve your spelling is to practise! Silent and unstressed letters are designed to trick you, so you need to be aware of these tricky little letters!

Try and group words based on shared letters. This will help you to identify how you would pronounce the word. For example, the words 'weigh' 'neigh' and 'sleigh' all use the letters 'eigh', and this helps to know how to pronounce the word. Of course, some words are tricky and would be pronounced differently.

REMEMBER = I before E except after C, but only when the sound is EE!

Any words that you have trouble spelling, write them down and remember to revise these.

Make sure you understand how to spell words based on the context in which they are being used. For example, the words 'maybe' and 'may be' are completely different!

Brush up on your vocabulary. Reading new words and understanding their definition is a great way to learn the meaning of the word and how to use it in writing.

Pay attention to tricky words that sound the same, but have different meanings. For example, 'affect' and 'effect' or 'practice' and 'practise'.

Make sure you know the difference between WHO, WHOM and WHOSE.

Make sure you know the difference between WHO, WHICH and THAT.

Question 1

How does the letter 'e' change the word 'hat'?

_____

_____

Question 2

What rule is broken with the words 'weird' and 'neighbour'?

_____

_____

Question 3

For the following sentences, circle the correct spelling of the word.

a) Maximus has basketball *(practise,   practice)* tonight.

b) We walked *(passed,   past)* the museum.

c) Eating too many sweets can *(effect,   affect)* your health.

d) She could not *(accept,   except)* the truth.

e) Is there *(anyway,   any way)* I can pay in instalments?

Question 4

Write the letter that is silent in the following words.

Thumb	Wrist	Numb	Climbing
_____	_____	_____	_____
Rhythm	Knew	Butcher	Wednesday
_____	_____	_____	_____
Guilty	Column	Wedge	Sign
_____	_____	_____	_____

Question 5

Complete the crossword below.

Across

2. Plural of thief

4. Homophone of by

5. I have judo (practice/practise)

7. Homophone of passed

8. Vowel sounds can _____ when you add an 'e' at the end

9. Word containing 'ay' sound, and used to describe how heavy someone is

Down

1. Letters you cannot hear

3. _____ vowels and long vowels

6. Lack of exercise will have a bad (affect/effect)

7. A rule or truth that serves as a system of belief

ANSWERS TO IMPROVING YOUR SPELLING

Question 1

The letter 'e' changes the word 'hat' to 'hate. By adding the 'e', this changes the vowel sound from 'a' to 'ay'.

Question 2

The rule that is broken with the words 'weird' and 'neighbour' is the rule: ' before E except after C, but only when the sound is EE!' The words 'weird' and 'neighbour' do not contain the letter 'C' and does not contain the sound 'EE'. Instead, 'weird' has the sound 'EAR' and the word 'neighbour' has the 'AY' sound.

Question 3

a) Maximus has basketball *practice* tonight.

b) We walked *past* the museum.

c) Eating too many sweets can *affect* your health.

d) She could not *accept* the truth.

e) Is there *any way* I can pay in instalments?

Question 4

Thumb	Wrist	Numb	Climbing
b	**w**	**b**	**b**
Rhythm	Knew	Butcher	Wednesday
h	**k**	**t**	**d**
Guilty	Column	Wedge	Sign
u	**n**	**d**	**g**

Question 5

Across

2. Plural of thief **THIEVES**

4. Homophone of by **BYE**

5. I have judo (practice/practise) **PRACTICE**

7. Homophone of passed **PAST**

8. Vowel sounds can _____ when you add an 'e' at the end **CHANGE**

9. Word containing 'ay' sound, and used to describe how heavy someone is **WEIGHT**

Down

1. Letters you cannot hear **SILENT**

3. _____ vowels and long vowels **SHORT**

6. Lack of exercise will have a bad **EFFECT**

7. A rule or truth that serves as a system of belief **PRINCIPLE**

THE
REVISION
SERIES

SINGULAR AND PLURALS

(Spelling)

SINGULARS AND PLURALS

SINGULAR ⟹ meaning **ONE**

PLURAL ⟹ meaning **MORE THAN ONE**

Plurals can be quite tricky if you do not know the basic rules when trying to convert a singular word to plural.

There are lots of different rules, and these all depend on what the word ends in.

Below is a list of the common rules you need to know to change a singular word to its plural word.

NOUNS	CHANGING IT TO PLURAL	EXAMPLES
For most nouns	Add 's'	Kites, dogs, cats, boats, lions
For most nouns ending in *ch, sh, s, x* or *z*	Add 'es'	Boxes, prizes, churches, banishes
For most nouns ending in a vowel (*a, e, i, o, u*) and *y*	Add 's'	days, boys, keys
For most nouns ending in a consonant and *y*	*Y* becomes 'ies'	Babies, countries, spies, puppies, berries
For most nouns ending in *f* or *fe*	*F* or *fe* becomes 'ves'	Wolves, wives, shelves
For most nouns ending in a vowel and an *o*	Add 's'	Zoos, kangaroos, radios
For most nouns ending in a consonant and *o*	Add 'es'	Heroes, potatoes, volcanoes

SINGULARS AND PLURALS

SOME WORDS DO NOT CHANGE

Some words have the same singular and plural. Both of them can either mean one or multiple.

| SHEEP | FISH | MUSIC | OFFSPRING |

IRREGULAR PLURALS

When you change some words into their plurals, sometimes the spelling of the word changes. Sometimes the vowel is changed to a different vowel, in order to make it plural.

Other times, extra letters are added to make the word plural. For example the plural of '*child*' is '*children*'. See how the letters '*ren*' are added.

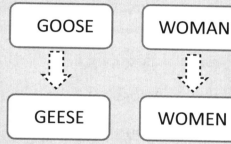
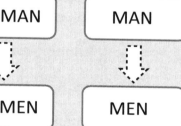
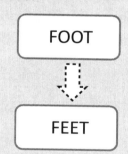

GOOSE	WOMAN	MAN	FOOT
⬇	⬇	⬇	⬇
GEESE	WOMEN	MEN	FEET

Some words are exceptions to the rules mentioned above. You need to pay attention to these unique words!

GAME! Why not get a friend or family member to write down lots of singular words, and then give yourself 5/10 minutes to write down their plurals. Practice makes perfect!

Question 1

Write the plural of the following words:

a) Ox

_____

b) Mouse

_____

c) Daisy

_____

d) Thief

_____

Question 2

Below are 6 categories. Place the words under the correct category to show how the word would change from its singular to plural.

CITY	ARMY	LADY	CHICK	BODY
DAY	CHILD	MAN	ELF	STORY
FISH	BUSH	DUCK	SPY	COUNTRY

ADD 'S'	ADD 'ES'	ADD 'IES'

ADD 'VES'	DON'T CHANGE	IRREGULAR

Question 3

To make a word ending in 'f' or 'fe' plural, you would often need to remove those letters and replace it with 'ves'.

However, there are exceptions to this rule. Give two words to demonstrate when this rule DOES NOT apply.

EXAMPLE 1

_____

EXAMPLE 2

_____

Question 4

Using the singular words below, write a sentence using its plural word instead. Remember to pay attention to spelling.

a) Celebrity

_____

b) Penguin

_____

c) Wolf

_____

d) Hero

_____

e) Rhino

_____

f) Deer

_____

ANSWERS TO SINGULAR AND PLURALS

Question 1
a) Oxen
b) Mice
c) Daisies
d) Thieves

Question 2
Add 's' = chick, day, duck
Add 'es' = bush
Add 'ies' = city, army, lady, body, story, spy, country
Add 'ves' = elf
Don't change = fish
Irregular = child, man

Question 3
You could have picked any word that ends in 'f' or 'fe', which doesn't change its spelling to 'ves'.

For example:

Beliefs, chiefs, roofs, chefs

Question 4
You could have wrote any sentence, so long as you have used the correct spelling of the plural for each word.

The spelling for each word would be as follows:

a) Celebrities
b) Penguins
c) Wolves
d) Heroes
e) Rhinos
f) Deer

HOW ARE YOU GETTING ON?

THE
REVISION
SERIES

PREFIXES AND SUFFIXES

(Spelling)

PREFIXES

PREFIXES: a letter or group of letters that you can add to the <u>beginning</u> of words in order to change their meanings.

PREFIX	EXAMPLES
Pre -	*Preview, precaution, preface*
Re -	*Retry, reabsorb, redo, realign*
Auto -	*Autobiography, autograph*
Un -	*Unhappy, unable, undeniable*
De -	*Debrief, deactivate, decode*
Sub -	*Subculture, submarine*
Trans -	*Transport, transcribe, transform*
In -	*Inactive, inability, inescapable*
Dis -	*Dismantle, disarm, disagree*
Im -	*Impossible, impolite, impatient*
Ir -	*Irregular, Irresponsible, irrational*
Il -	*Illogical, illegal, illiterate*

A **PREFIX** is added to the **BEGINNING** of a **ROOT** word in order to create a new word. (PRE = before)

PREFIXES often make the **ROOT** word have an **OPPOSITE MEANING**. For example, adding the prefix 'in' to 'active' makes it take the opposite meaning. Active becomes inactive.

The spelling of root words **NEVER** change. This may result in double letters in the word. For example, unnecessary has two 'nn'. You should never delete or add in letters to the root word.

SUFFIXES

SUFFIXES are letters that can be added to the <u>end</u> of a word in order to change its meaning.

SUFFIX	EXAMPLES
- Less	Hope**less**, power**less**, sense**less**
- Ment	Depart**ment**, pay**ment**, commit**ment**
- Er	Attack**er**, keep**er**, bounc**er**
- Ness	Effective**ness**, firm**ness**, ill**ness**
- Ity	Abnormal**ity**, credibil**ity**, objectiv**ity**
- Ly	Abrupt**ly**, amazing**ly**, bare**ly**
- Able	Account**able**, unavoid**able**, break**able**
- Ful	Bash**ful**, delight**ful**, forget**ful**
- Ing	Allow**ing**, tim**ing**, jump**ing**, build**ing**
- Ed	Abandon**ed**, adapt**ed**, encourag**ed**
- Ise	Criti**cise**, familiar**ise**, global**ise**
- Ible	Access**ible**, destruct**ible**, revers**ible**

A **SUFFIX** is added to the **END** of a **ROOT** word in order to create a new word.

SUFFIXES can change verbs and adjectives into nouns by adding *ment, ness, er* or *ity*.

Suffixes can turn verbs and nouns into adjectives by adding *less, ful, ible* and *able*.

Suffixes can turn adjectives into adverbs by adding *ly*. They can also change nouns and adjectives into verbs by adding *ify* or *ise*.

Question 1

For each prefix or suffix, use it in a word.

_____FUL   _____LESS   _____ED   _____ING

_____LY   _____ABLE   _____ER   _____EST

OVER_____   DIS_____   PRE_____   MIS_____

RE_____   IM_____   UN_____   BI_____

Question 2

Give a definition of suffixes.

_____

_____

_____

Question 3

Give a definition of prefixes.

_____

_____

_____

Question 4

Complete the prefix or suffix using the words below. Can you find them in the word search?

> LOGICAL   FUNCTION   SMALL   QUIET   APPROPRIATE
>
> APPRENTICE   VISION   COLD   REGULAR   ACCEPT   REAL
>
> MOBILE   ACT   CARE   CYCLE   ACHIEVE

BI_____   AUTO_____   _____ION   MAL_____

_____EST   _____LY   _____LESS   IN_____

UNDER_____   SUPER_____   _____NESS   _____ABLE

IL_____   IR_____   _____SHIP   _____ITY

```
A U T O M O B I L E N A I N S
A T T E Q Q N S W O R P L O S
L C W S V U S E I Y E P L I E
J U C O E E I S U A A R O T L
J R G E N L I E P E L E G C E
U H P D P V L H T C I N I N R
M Y L M R T B A C L T T C U A
A O H E Q G A X M A Y T A F C
C S P N M R I B G S R C L L W
A U X B I C Y C L E C E U A B
S N O I T C A T R E T S D M B
R A L U G E R R I C Z H E N B
M W S D O V G P H W C I P V U
R I E T A I R P O R P P A N I
A M H K N B M C V G Y R H Q N
```

ANSWERS TO PREFIXES AND SUFFIXES

Question 1

You could have used any word you wanted, so long as the prefix or suffix can be used with that word. Get a parent or teacher to check your answers to this question.

<u>For example:</u>

Respectful, fearless, jumped, talking, slowly, unable, shorter, smallest, overachieve, disregard, premature, misinterpret, recycle, impolite, unattractive, bicycle

Question 2

Suffixes are groups of letters that you can add to the end of the word in order to change its meaning.

Question 3

Prefixes are letters or groups of letters which you can add to the beginning of a word in order to change its meaning.

Question 4

Bicycle, automobile, malfunction, action, smallest, quietly, careless, inappropriate, underachieve, supervision, coldness, acceptable, illogical, irregular, apprenticeship, reality

HOW ARE YOU GETTING ON?

THE
REVISION
SERIES

HOMOPHONES AND HOMONYMS

(Spelling)

HOMONYMS

HOMOPHONES are words that <u>sound the same</u>, but have **DIFFERENT** meanings and spellings.

NEAR HOMOPHONES are words that don't really sound the same, but are commonly misspelt. For example, affect and effect, access or excess.

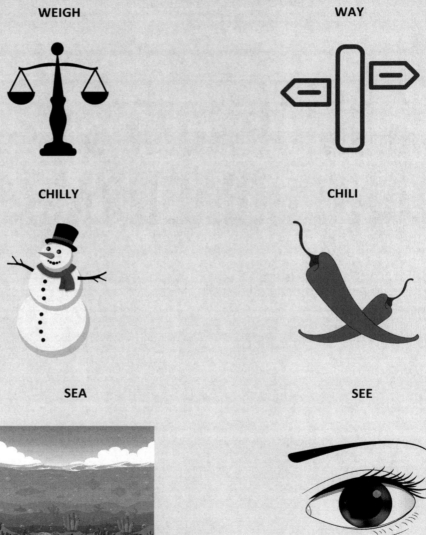

WEIGH

WAY

CHILLY

CHILI

SEA

SEE

What other words can you think of that are SPELT DIFFERENTLY and have DIFFERENT MEANINGS?

HOMONYMS are words that are spelt the **SAME** but have **DIFFERENT** meanings.

Can you work out the homonyms shown by these pictures?

PARK (a playground)

PARK (a car)

FIRE (a house fire)

FIRE (a gun)

BARK (sound of a dog)

BARK (of a tree)

How many other words can you think of that are SPELT THE SAME but have DIFFERENT MEANINGS?

Question 1

Below is a list of homonyms. In the space provided, write down two different meanings of how that word can be used.

HOMONYM	MEANING 1	MEANING 2
Ring		
Rock		
Row		
Duck		
Chest		

Question 2

Below is a list of homophones. In the space provided, write down two different meanings of how that word can be used.

HOMOPHONE	Alternative Spelling
Which	
Waste	
Sale	
Knew	
Heard	
Berry	

Question 3

Explain what **near homophones** are, and provide two examples.

_____

_____

_____

EXAMPLE 1

_____

EXAMPLE 2

_____

Question 4

Explain what **homonyms** are.

_____

_____

_____

Question 5

Explain what **homophones** are.

_____

_____

_____

Question 6

The following sentences are incorrect. Underline the word/s that is incorrec
and write the correct spelling of the word/s.

a) Mia had to go and see the principle to discuss her behaviour.

_____

b) I had serial for breakfast.

_____

c) It was difficult to drive because of the missed.

_____

d) The too boys spent there day playing video games.

_____

ANSWERS TO HOMOPHONES AND HOMONYMS

Question 1

HOMONYM	MEANING 1	MEANING 2
Ring	A ring you wear on your finger.	A boxing ring
Rock	A large stone.	A movement – to move back and forth in a rocking motion (i.e. a rocking chair)
Row	An argument.	A row of seats (line of seats).
Duck	An animal.	To 'duck' down.
Chest	A treasure chest.	Part of the body.

Question 2

HOMOPHONE	Alternative Spelling
Which	Witch
Waste	Waist
Sale	Sail
Knew	New
Heard	Herd
Berry	Bury

Question 3

Near homophones are words that do not actually sound the same, but the are commonly misspelt because they are quite similar.

Example 1 – edition and addition **Example 2** – accept and except

(Other examples you could have given include advise and advice, affect and effect. If you have any others, please get a teacher or parent to check then for you).

Question 4

Homonyms are words that look and sound the same, but have a differen meaning. If you used the word, it could be used in different contexts, and tha context is usually obvious to the reader.

Question 5

Homophones are words that sound the same, but have different meanings and spellings.

Question 6

a) Mia had to go and see the <u>principle</u> to discuss her behaviour

PRINCIPAL

b) I had <u>serial</u> for breakfast.

CEREAL

c) It was difficult to drive because of <u>missed</u>.

MIST

d) The <u>too</u> boys spent <u>there</u> day playing video games.

TWO and **THEIR**

HOW ARE YOU GETTING ON?

THE
REVISION
SERIES

ACTIVE AND PASSIVE SENTENCES

(Sentence Structure)

ACTIVE AND PASSIVE SENTENCES

When it comes to writing sentences, there are two types of voices that you need to be aware of:

* Active voice
* Passive voice

ACTIVE VOICE

The active voice is the most '*normal*' voice that is used when creating sentences.

The active voice focuses on the subject doing the action. It is made obvious who is doing the action.

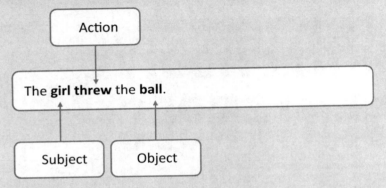

PASSIVE VOICE

The passive voice tells us that something or someone has an action done to them.

The passive voice focuses on 'what' as opposed to 'who' – something is done to the subject.

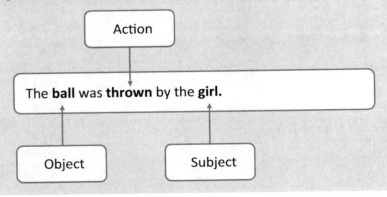

Question 1

Explain the difference between an active voice and a passive voice.

_____

_____

_____

Question 2

Write three example sentences for **passive voice**.

a) _____

b) _____

c) _____

Question 3

Write three example sentences for **active voice**.

a) _____

b) _____

c) _____

Question 4

Rewrite the following sentences, changing the active voice into passive voice.

a) The doctor removed my appendix

_____

_____

b) The school arranged a school trip.

_____

_____

c) The thunderstorm woke my baby brother up.

_____

_____

Question 5

Rewrite the following sentences, changing the passive voice into active voice.

a) A report about finances was written by my dad.

_____

_____

b) The football tournament was cancelled due to the torrential downpour.

_____

_____

c) The playhouse was built in my back garden by my friend in less than two weeks.

_____

_____

ANSWERS TO ACTIVE AND PASSIVE SENTENCES

Question 1

Active sentences focus on who is doing the action, and there is a clear link between the subject and the object. The passive voice focuses on 'what' as opposed to 'whom'; it focuses on something being done to the subject.

Question 2

You can write any three sample sentences so long as you use the passive voice. Get a parent or teacher to check these for you.

Examples –

a) The squirrel was being chased by the dog.

b) A pond was built by John.

c) The sandwich was stolen by Fredrick.

Question 3

You can write any three sample sentences so long as you use the active voice. Get a parent or teacher to check these for you.

Examples –

a) The dog chased the squirrel.

b) John built a pond.

c) Frederick stole the sandwich.

Question 4

a) My appendix was removed by the doctor.

b) A school trip was arranged by the school.

c) My baby brother was woken up by the thunderstorm.

Question 5

a) My dad wrote a report about finances.

b) The torrential downpour caused the football tournament to be cancelled

c) In less than two weeks, my friend built a playhouse in my back garden.

THE
REVISION
SERIES

SENTENCES, CLAUSES AND PHRASES

(Sentence Structure)

SENTENCES, CLAUSES AND PHRASES

Now that you have a good understanding of grammar and spelling, it is time to tackle sentence structure.

SENTENCES

A sentence is made up of a group of words in order to form a:

- Statement
- Question
- Exclamation
- Command

(For more information on these, please check out the Grammar section of this book.)

A sentence must contain a verb, and should make sense on its own.

A simple sentence is called a **clause**.

MAIN CLAUSES

A clause is a sentence that contains a verb and a subject.

Every sentence contains a **main clause**. It is the <u>main idea</u> of the sentence, which works on its own as a simple sentence.

> I am a fisherman.

Some sentences contain **two main clauses**. You will know whether they are both main clauses, because they will be of equal importance, and would be able to stand as two separate sentences.

Two main clauses in a sentence is a **COMPOUND SENTENCE**.

> I am a fisherman and my sister is a dentist.

Main clauses are usually joined by **conjunction words** *(See the conjunction section for more information.)*

SENTENCES, CLAUSES AND PHRASES

COMPLEX SENTENCES

More <u>complex sentences</u> will join a **main clause** to a **subordinate clause**.

A **SUBORDINATE CLAUSE** will contain the <u>main clause</u> and a <u>less important clause</u>.

Subordinate clauses do not make sense on their own.

> Sammie came home from school, *an hour late*, and almost missed saying goodbye to his dad.

- *'An hour late'* does not make sense on its own.
- It is adding extra information to the main clause.

Subordinate clauses usually begin with the words:
- Because
- While
- Until

RELATIVE CLAUSES

A **RELATIVE CLAUSE** is another type of a <u>subordinate clause</u> which <u>adds extra information</u>.

The extra information ultimately adapts, describes or modifies a <u>noun</u>.

Relative clauses use **relative pronouns** to introduce the clause, such as:
- That
- Which
- Who
- Whose

> Mikey, *who was caught stealing*, was grounded by his parents.

Relative pronouns do not always have to be written in order for the sentence to be a relative clause. You can sometime remove the relative pronoun, and it would still make sense.

SENTENCES, CLAUSES AND PHRASES

PHRASES are parts of sentences, which usually DO NOT have a verb.

Sometimes, it may have a verb, but there will be no one doing the verb.

Jessie drives the car <u>around the rally track.</u>

- The underlined part of the sentence is a **PHRASE**.
- This part of the sentence does not contain a verb.
- The first part of the sentence (Jessie drives the car) is a clause. It contains a verb and a subject.

MAIN CLAUSES are main ideas. They work on their own as a simple sentence.

TWO MAIN CLAUSES make up a **COMPOUND SENTENCE**.

COMPLEX SENTENCES are made up of a main clause and a subordinate clause.

SUBORDINATE CLAUSE contains a main clause and a less important clause.

PHRASES are parts of sentences that usually do not contain a verb. If it does contain a verb, there will be no subject.

Question 1

Write the definition of the following:

Main clause

_____

_____

_____

Subordinate clause

_____

_____

_____

Relative clause

_____

_____

_____

Compound sentence

_____

_____

_____

Question 2

Tick the box to say whether the bold statement is a **main clause** o
subordinate clause.

Sentence	Main Clause	Subordinate clause
The boy, **who was eight**, fell over.		
My sister (who was turning 21) **was having a party**.		
The stolen vehicle sped along the motorway, which was chased by two police cars.		
We can go to the cinema, **unless you don't feel well enough.**		

Question 3

Complete the crossword below.

Across

3. Relative _____ can be used to introduce relative clauses.

4. A type of sentence that is made up of a main clause and a less important clause.

6. A type of clause that is less important than a main clause.

Down

1. A type of sentence that contains two main clauses.

2. A part of a sentence, usually without a verb.

5. A type of word used to join two main clauses.

7. A type of subordinate clause that gives extra information about a noun.

Question 4

Rewrite the sentence and add relative clauses to make the sentences descriptive.

a) Mia and Ellie were playing in the park.

_____

b) During the summer holidays, I went to the zoo.

_____

c) I fell off my bike.

_____

Question 5

Rewrite the two sentences using a conjunction in order to create a complex sentence.

a) The student wrote a short story.　　The teacher thought it was brilliant.

_____

b) You should sort out your clothes.　　Your wardrobe is overflowing.

_____

c) I was emptying the dishwasher.　　My brother hoovered the floor.

_____

ANSWERS TO SENTENCES, CLAUSES AND PHRASES

Question 1

Main clause

Every sentence contains a main clause. The main clause is the main idea of the sentence, which works on its own as a simple sentence.

Subordinate clause

A subordinate clause will contain the main clause and a less important clause.

Relative clause

A relative clause is a type of subordinate clause that provides added information about a noun.

Compound sentence

A compound sentence is made up of two main clauses. Each of these clauses would be able to work as a sentence on its own. Both sentences are of equal importance.

Question 2

Sentence	Main Clause	Subordinate clause
The boy, **who was eight**, fell over.		✔
My sister (who was turning 21) **was having a party**.	✔	
The stolen vehicle sped along the motorway, which was chased by two police cars.	✔	
We can go to the cinema, **unless you don't feel well enough**.		✔

Question 3

Across

3. Relative _____ can be used to introduce relative clauses. **PRONOUNS**

4. A type of sentence that is made up of a main clause and a less important clause. **COMPLEX**

6. A type of clause that is less important than a main clause. **SUBORDINATE**

Down

1. A type of sentence that contains two main clauses. **COMPOUND**

2. A part of a sentence, usually without a verb. **PHRASE**

5. A type of word used to join two main clauses. **CONJUNCTION**

7. A type of subordinate clause that gives extra information about a noun. **RELATIVE**

Question 4

a) Mia and Ellie were playing in the park, and were having a great time.

b) During the summer holidays, I went to the zoo, which is my favourite place.

c) I fell off my bike, and scratched my leg.

Question 5

a) The student wrote a short story **and** the teacher thought it was brilliant.

b) You should sort out your clothes **because** your wardrobe is overflowing.

c) I was emptying the dishwasher **whilst** my brother hoovered the floor.

HOW ARE YOU GETTING ON?

NEED A LITTLE EXTRA HELP WITH KEY STAGE THREE (KS3) ENGLISH?

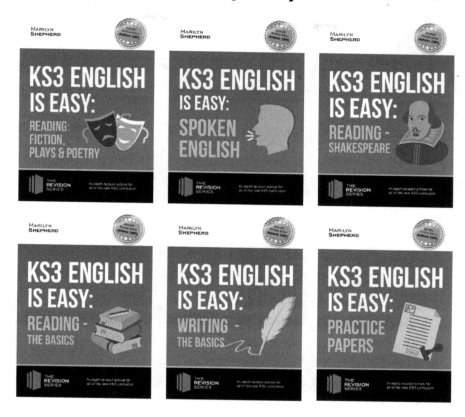

How2become have created these other FANTASTIC guides to help you and your child prepare for their Key Stage Three (KS3) English assessments.

These exciting guides are filled with fun and interesting facts for your child to engage with to ensure that their revision is fun, and their learning is improved! Invest in your child's future today!

FOR MORE INFORMATION ON OUR KEY STAGE 3 (KS3) GUIDES, PLEASE CHECK OUT THE FOLLOWING:

WWW.HOW2BECOME.COM

Get Access To

FREE

Psychometric Tests

www.PsychometricTestsOnline.co.uk

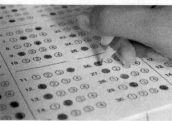